Lighthouses of the
Dry Tortugas,
An Illustrated History

By Neil E. Hurley

𝔥istoric 𝔏ighthouse 𝔓ublishers
Aiea, Hawaii

Lighthouses
of the Dry Tortugas
An Illustrated History
By Neil E. Hurley

Copyright 1994 by Neil E. Hurley
Third Printing 2002

All rights reserved. No part of this book may be copied without the author's permission.

Printed in the United States of America
By Historic Lighthouse Publishers
ISCB: 0-945172-31-1

Additional copies of this book may be ordered from the publisher by e-mailing:
lthouse@erols.com

Contents

A Dangerous Obstacle 1

Building the Lighthouse 5

A Hard Life 9

The Wreck of the AMERICA 15

Temporary Fixes 19

New Neighbors and the Great Escape 23

A New Light 29

The Fort Becomes a Prison 35

Hurricanes and Repairs 39

Quiet Times Despite War 43

The End of an Era 47

Flashing Lights 53

Garden Key Today 61

Loggerhead Key Today 65

Photo Credits 72
Footnotes 73
The Author 78
Index 79

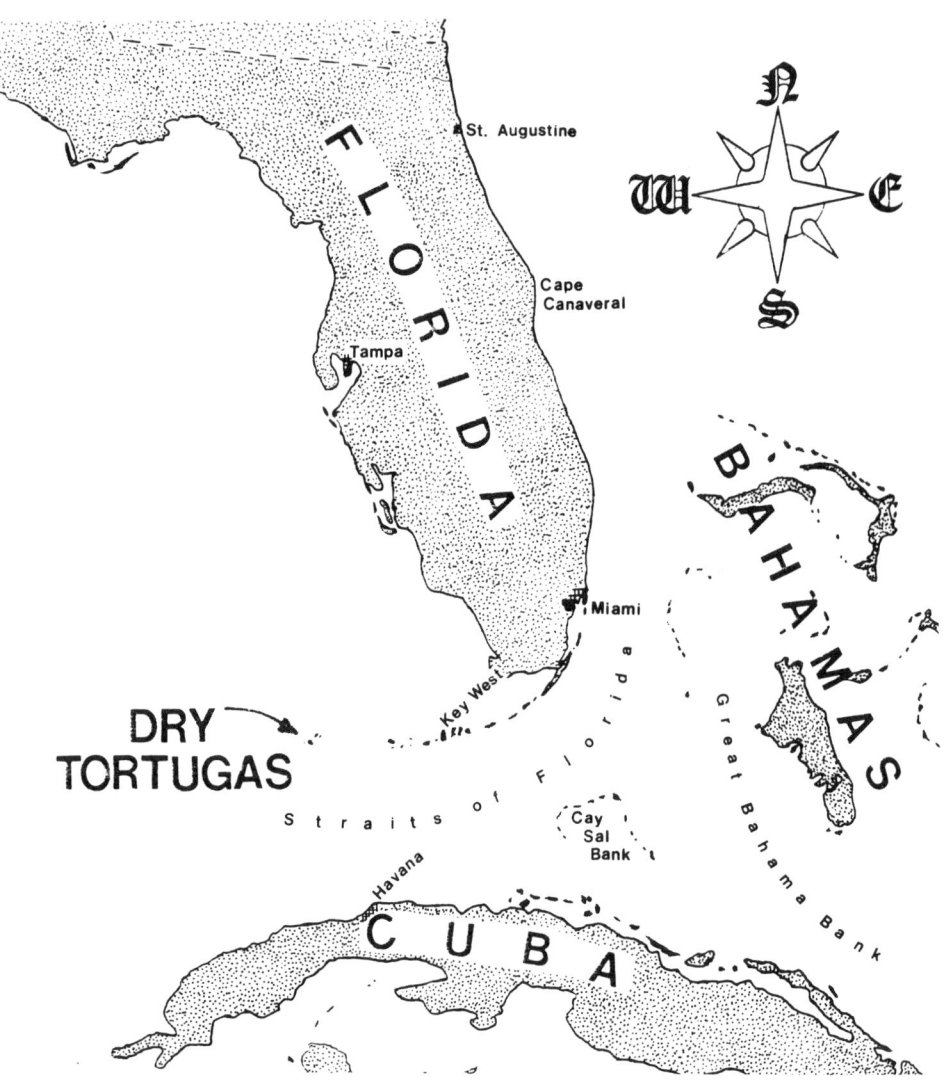

The Dry Tortugas and Straits of Florida. One eighteenth century report stated "all (ed. of the numerous rocks and reefs of the area) could be covered with the inscriptions of the many who ended their Navigations on it".

A Dangerous Obstacle

Far distant islands, surrounded by perilous reefs and topaz blue waters. This is what faced Juan Ponce de Leon in 1513.[1]* It certainly wouldn't have been an impressive landfall. Only seven to ten keys, depending if you count seasonal sandbars, totaling a scant 80 acres.[2] Passages between the reefs are not obvious, and the deep-water paths to the islands are full of twists and turns. When de Leon's crews captured 160 sea turtles in one night, it made the name of the island group obvious. He named them the "Tortugas", the Spanish word for turtle.[1]

Situated at the westernmost tip of the Florida Keys, the Dry Tortugas represent the last obstacle for ships going through the Straits of Florida. Besides marking an important turning point for ships bound from the Atlantic to the northern Gulf of Mexico, a deep-water channel just east of the Dry Tortugas provides a shortcut for vessels bound for the west coast of Florida. Changing currents and eddies of the Gulf Stream, low fogs and the ever present danger of hurricanes have resulted in nearly 200 documented shipwrecks and strandings, of which over one-third were total losses.[3]

In late 1565 the Englishman John Hawkins stopped at the Tortugas during his second trip to the New World to lay in supplies for his

*footnote citations are listed starting on page 73

trip back to Spain. Taking a small pinnace into one of the islands, he "found such a number of birds, that in half an hour he loaded her with them, and if there had been 10 boats more, they might have done the like". They also took many turtles which, to them, tasted like veal. Hawkins' fleet anchored at the Tortugas only six hours, leaving because of a strong wind and also to look for fresh water.[4] On his third voyage, Hawkins' fleet of eight ships ran into two hurricanes off the Florida keys. Forced by storm damage into a Mexican port, he was later captured by the Spanish.[5]

The area's first recorded shipwreck occurred in 1621 when a small unidentified Spanish ship was capsized and sunk by a huge wave about nine miles off the Tortugas. Thirty of the crew drowned, but some survivors reached shore where they built signal fires. The fires were seen by another Spanish ship and the survivors were rescued. The following year, the Spanish galleon NUESTRA SENORA DEL ROSARIO was wrecked at the Dry Tortugas in a hurricane. Its treasure of silver bars and coins valued at 500,000 pesos was recovered by Spanish salvors from Havana, Cuba. Another seven ships were recorded as lost in the Dry Tortugas in the incomplete records kept before 1824.[3]

Ships from other nations were also on the prowl for Spanish gold and silver. From 1624 until 1640, Dutch fleets gathered at the Dry Tortugas to prey on Spanish treasure fleets. In 1628, the largest gathering occurred when a Dutch fleet of 35 ships and 4,000 men put in to the islands.[6]

A detailed survey of the islands was conducted by the Englishman George Gauld in 1773. He identified ten islets: North, Sand, East, Bird, Middle, Long, Bush, Booby, Turtle and Southwest Keys. Turtle and Bush Keys are known today as Loggerhead and Garden Keys.[7]

The name of the islands was changed to "Dry Tortugas" well before they became American territory. Most sources state that "dry" refers to the lack of fresh water on the islands, but one source from 1868 says "Dry they were called in contradistinction to the vast tract of wet reef which at low-water nearly reaches to the surface."[8]

The first lighthouse planned for the Dry Tortugas was one of two twin towers designed by William De Brahm, the Surveyor General of East Florida, while Florida was a British territory. The two lighthouses were part of a proposal made to King George III in

1773. De Brahm reported that the Spanish treasure fleets used the Florida Straits as well as "a great number of English vessels which trade in the Gulf of Mexico". Although the area was covered by many rocks and reefs "all could be covered with the Inscriptions of the many who ended their Navigations on it." To end the terrible shipping losses, De Brahm proposed building two huge lighthouses (De Brahm called them "Pharuses" after the famous ancient Egyptian lighthouse) "to mark the passage between the island of Cuba and the promontory of East Florida ... one on the east, and one on the west extremity of the promontory." Although De Brahm wasn't specific, he probably intended the sites to be Cape Florida (on Key Biscayne) and the Dry Tortugas. The towers would be named George and Charlotte after the King of England and his wife, Charlotte Sophia.

The towers proposed by De Brahm were huge: 260 feet tall (16 stories) with an eight-sided fortress-like stone base and a six-sided wooden tower. The base was designed to hold 24 cannon, with another 6 cannon in the tower. Up to 450 soldiers could be quartered in wartime. Five hundred steps would lead to the top where a railed-in platform would contain a stove and a flagpole. The stove (made of either iron or brick) would be constantly lit to provide a smoke signal for ships during the day and a light at night. "Sky rockets" would be fired each half hour at night as an additional signal. One surprising omission in De Brahm's plan was a means of providing the large quantities of wood or coal to the stove at the top of the tower. The choice of a stove probably reflected De Brahm's ignorance of lighthouse technology, as more effective and fuel efficient means were in use elsewhere.

De Bram's lighthouse of 1773

Each lighthouse would have a sloop and a barge (an oared vessel) to carry shipping pilots and to assist wrecked ships. When a ship was sighted, the lookouts would dip the flag at the lighthouse top as a signal to the ship and to a sentry at the base of the tower. The sentry would wake a drummer, who in turn would call out a gun crew. The firing of a gun would signal the pilot boat to make sail.

King George's reaction to De Brahm's plan wasn't recorded. Apparently it was unfavorable, since De Brahm's later reports fail to mention the lighthouses. Whether it was the huge expense of building and maintaining the towers, or the growing restlessness of the American Colonies (the Boston Tea Party occurred the year before), nothing ever came of De Brahm's proposal.

Except for the Statue of Liberty (total height 291 feet and administered as a lighthouse from its dedication in 1886 until 1902) no western hemisphere lighthouse has yet approached the size of De Brahm's towers. Had they been built, they would have been America's greatest lighthouses. The Dry Tortugas remained unlit for another 53 years, claiming dozens more shipwrecks.[9]

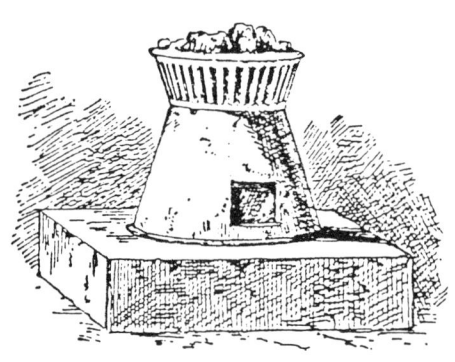

A design for an early lighthouse stove.

Building the Lighthouse

In 1819, the King of Spain sold Florida to the United States for five million dollars.[8] Reports of the danger of the Florida reefs and of the Dry Tortugas' reefs in particular had been well documented. An 1823 report said that with a good man on lookout at the masthead, all the heads and shoals could be seen "a good way off" during the daytime in fair weather. The 1822 "American Coast Pilot" warned that sailors should not approach closer to the Dry Tortugas than two miles, as there were "some rocky spits" extending that distance from shore. But it also warned, "if safe by day", the reef was not so at night or in bad weather. Captains were warned to keep the lead lines going in order to stay clear of the dangerous reef.[3]

Because of the high number of shipwrecks in the area, Congress appropriated funds for four lighthouses in South Florida on May 26, 1824.[10] Three lighthouses, at Cape Florida, Sambo Keys (later built at Key West) and the Dry Tortugas, were contracted for on July 31, 1824 (a lightship was later contracted for on Carysfort Reef). The contract was awarded to Samuel B. Lincoln of Boston. His winning bid was for $29,847.

The contract called for "The tower to be built of stone or hard brick, the form round ... The height of the tower to be sixty five feet from the surface of the ground, the diameter of the base to be twenty five feet, and that of the top twelve feet, the thickness of the walls at the base to be five feet, to be uniformly graduated to two feet at the top. The top to be arched on which to be laid a deck of soap stone, fourteen and a half feet in diameter, five inches thick, the joints filled in with lead, on one side of which to be a scuttle twenty four by twenty inches, to enter the lantern, the scuttle door an iron frame covered with copper ... There are to be six windows in the tower of twelve lights each, of ten by eight glass, in strong frames, and a door five feet by three feet; made of double inch boards, cross nailed, with substantial hinges, lock and latch. The ground floor to be paved with brick or stone. A sufficient number of circular stairs to lead from the ground floor to within six feet of the lantern, connected by a center post, guarded by a good hand railing ... of good Georgia pine, free of sap ... On top to be an iron lantern of an octagon form, the posts to be two inches square, to run down five feet into the stone or brick work and secured with anchors. The height and diameter of the lantern to be sufficient to admit an iron sash in each octagon, to contain twenty one lights, of fourteen by twelve glass, the lower tier to be fitted with copper. The rabbits of the sashes to be three quarters of an inch deep and glazed with double glass, from the Boston manufactory. In one of the Octagons to be an iron frame door covered with copper, four feet by two in the clear, to shut tight into the rabbets with a strong turned button, the top to be a dome, formed by sixteen iron rafters ... covered with copper". The dwelling house, 34 by 20, was to be made of brick. The downstairs contained two rooms with a chimney in the middle with two bedrooms upstairs. A porch, kitchen and well or cistern completed the structures, but the contract also contained the lighting apparatus including lamps, reflectors, tin oil butts, wick boxes, tube boxes, a hand lantern, torch files, and scissors.[11]

Just before construction started on the lighthouse (December 1825), Commodore David Porter examined the Dry Tortugas considering it as a possible site for a naval station. He reported back that the Tortugas was totally unfit for any kind of naval base. He reported they "consist of small sand Islands a little above the surface of the Ocean, on some of which is some low shrubbery, but all are liable to changes from gales of wind. Their insulated situation, and distance from the continent renders blockade easy; they have a good inner harbor for small craft and a tolerable outer one for ships of war; but they have no fresh water, and furnish scarcely land enough to place a fortification and it is doubtful if they have solidity enough to bear one."[8]

Meanwhile, Lincoln gathered materials in Boston and set sail in August 1824. His ship sank along the way, apparently with no survivors, as he was never heard from again. Lincoln's backers were allowed to take over the contract and a new completion deadline was set. A second ship sent from Boston arrived safely on December 12, 1824. Work was begun first on the lighthouse at

Key West, with work on the Dry Tortugas and Cape Florida lights beginning after February 8, 1825.[12] The actual site of the latter two lighthouses was fixed by Noah Humphries of Boston, who, as agent for the United States government, also oversaw construction of the lighthouses.

Work was suspended during the summer of 1825 due to "the general sickness of the workmen".[12] Construction was completed before April 1, 1826, but the light was not lit until July 4, 1826 due to the failure of the first keeper to arrive.[3,13]

The completed lighthouse had 23 lamps each with a 14 inch reflector and displayed a fixed (not flashing) light. The tower was constructed of brick which was whitewashed on the exterior.[14] The light tower was located on the eastern shore of Garden Key (then called Bush Key), closer to the deep water channel which ran along that side of the channel. The dwelling house was detached from the tower and stood just south of it.[15] Operation of the lighthouse was overseen by the Collector of Customs at Key West.

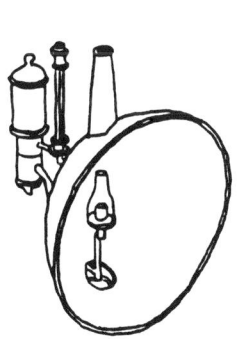 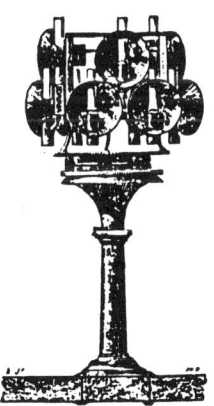

Lamps and reflectors of this type were originally used at the Dry Tortugas.

Turtle Turning

A valuable source of food and perhaps extra income for lighthouse keepers in the Dry Tortugas came from the capture of sea turtles. Three types of turtle were common at the Dry Tortugas. Hawksbill turtles had shells that were prized as raw materials for hair combs and jewelry. Green and Loggerhead turtles were prized for their meat, which could be boiled into turtle soup and their eggs.[16,17]

There were two principal ways to catch turtles. In the first, called pegging, the turtle was speared while in the water with a harpoon-like device. This usually killed the turtle, so it had to be eaten right away before the meat spoiled.[18]

Turning Turtles

A less destructive method of capture was called turtle turning. On moonlit summer nights female turtles come onshore to lay their eggs. If overturned while onshore, the turtle would be helpless and could later be retrieved for its shell and meat. The advantage here was that the turtle could be kept alive on its back for several weeks before it was eaten. No other meat could be stored "fresh" with so little care until refrigeration was invented. It was an ideal food for ship's crews.

Flipping a 300 pound Loggerhead turtle did have several drawbacks. Although they have a limited reach, sea turtles can bite. They can also deliver a wicked blow with their flippers. "To upset a turtle on the shore" wrote the famed naturalist John Audubon of his 1832 visit to the Tortugas, "one is obliged to fall on his knees, and, placing his shoulder behind her forearm, gradually raise her up by pushing with great force, and then with a jerk throw her over. Sometimes it requires the united strength of several men to accomplish this; and, if the turtle should be of very great size, as often happens on that coast, even handspikes are employed." Other reports from the 1860's recorded that turtle turning was considered to be exciting recreation.[19]

Many men also earned a living hunting turtle eggs. The eggs were located by walking the beaches until turtle tracks were found. The sand at the end of the tracks was probed with a wooden stick until the eggs were located. Turtle nests held as many as 200 eggs.

Overhunting of sea turtles brought them to the verge of extinction. Thanks to protected areas such as Fort Jefferson National Monument, sea turtles have a chance to escape extinction.

A Brown Pelican and sea gull struggle for food.

A Hard Life

The first lighthouse keeper was Major John L. Flaherty. He and his wife Rebecca came to the Dry Tortugas from the northern United States. Life for Flaherty and his family was a far cry from life back home. One early complaint stemmed from a small marshy pond close to the dwelling house. Brackish ponds were considered to cause sickness from the "malodorous" gases they gave off. In October 1826 the Collector of Customs requested authorization from Washington for the $15 expense of filling in the pond. Funds were approved at the same time for similar work at the lighthouses at Key West and Cape Florida.

Another concern (common with early lighthouse reflector systems) was noted with the equipment in the lighthouse tower. The reflectors were made of glass plated with silver, much like mirrors of today. The reflectors required frequent cleaning because of the ash and soot from the early lamps, but cleansers of those days were abrasive and quickly wore the silvering off. With no replacements available, the keepers were placed in a no-win situation. Either leave the lamps dirty, or reduce their reflectivity each time they were cleaned.[20]

In late October 1826, Flaherty wrote the Collector of Customs at Key West complaining about the quality of oil provided to the lighthouse under a contract from the Boston lighthouse chandler, Winslow Lewis. The Collector, William Pinkney, inspected the oil at Key West lighthouse and also found it to be bad.[21]

Soon after, the lighthouse was visited by the Revenue Cutter MARION from Charleston. On arriving at the lighthouse Mr.

Flaherty went over to the ship and reported that he was exhausted from his duties and needed help. First Officer Samuel Franklin went over in a boat and reported the lighthouse was "very dirty, the window glasses very black with soot, the lamps were stopped up with plugs of burnt wicks, some of the tubes were not on, some of the lamps had no wick, nor oil." Eight more men were sent over and by early evening the upper part, including the steps, was properly cleaned. They also cleaned all the lamps and reported that the light showed a brilliant light that night. The supplies transferred to the lighthouse sound as if Flaherty was expecting an invasion. They included a cutlass, a musket, two pistols, flints, rope, canvas, nails and a bucket.[22]

On finding that Flaherty wasn't doing his duty, Collector Pinkney investigated the situation. Flaherty had complained of poor provisions, mosquitoes and the poor condition of the dwelling. He interviewed Mrs. Flaherty and her sister but found that conditions on Garden Key were no worse than those at other locations on the Florida coast. The lighthouse had plenty of salted provisions, potatoes and live hogs. The pond would soon be filled in, reducing the numbers of mosquitoes and work to plaster the inside of the dwelling would soon be done. Pinkney recommended that the Flahertys be transferred to the new lighthouse at Sand Key. At that location, only 10 miles from Key West, Pinkney could keep a better watch on the lighthouse's operations and the Flaherty's supply problem would be eased.

Rebecca Flaherty also took matters into her own hands. At the end of November 1826 she wrote to the wife of President John Qunicy Adams.[23] Collector Pinkney replied to Washington saying "The lights upon this coast are well attended to, but Mr. Flaherty does not keep the Tortugas Light as well as I think he ought ... Permit me Sir, to mention that the Salary of the Keepers is too low. When the high prices they are compelled to pay for the necessaries of life are considered, to say nothing of the privations they undergo, surely $400 per annum is but a poor provision for them. I sincerely hope that further renumeration may be granted to them."[24] Apparently the letter worked, as in mid-January 1827 the President appointed Mr. Flaherty keeper of Sand Key light.[25] It wasn't until after the Flahertys left that the stagnant pond on Garden Key was finally filled in at a cost of $50.[26]

Flaherty's replacement at the Dry Tortugas was Joseph Himinez of St. Augustine, Florida. Among his attributes, it was cited that "his constitution is habituated to this climate, and that I think an important consideration."[27] Himinez was originally appointed to Sand Key lighthouse, but a trade was worked out to bring Flaherty closer to Key West. Himinez was one of only a very few keepers with a Spanish surname to serve in southern Florida.

Sand Key Light
Florida Reef

The Flaherty's at Sand Key

"I am glad to be able to report to you that the light on Sand Key was lit on the 15th inst (April 15, 1827) and that Mr. Flaherty keeps it in good order. This light is a remarkably fine one in all respects and the whole apparatus as well as the oil furnished is of superior quality." So wrote William Pinkney, the Collector of Customs at Key West, ending the complaints about John Flaherty as a lighthouse keeper.[26,28] In May 1828, Flaherty was granted a leave of absence to travel north *"for medical assistance in consequence of an injury he has sustained."*[28] He died three years later.

On her husband's death, Rebecca Flaherty took over the job of keeper.[29] Edward Van Evans of Key West took over the job of keeper after marrying Rebecca in 1833.[30] Rebecca remarried again in 1835 (Van Evans' fate is unclear) to a Captain Niell. This time she retained her position of lighthouse keeper as Captain Niell was frequently absent. One report stated *"Mrs. Niell is extremely attentive to her duties and since the (clock) works have been impaired has sat up nearly the whole of two nights turning the light by hand."*[31]

Joshua Appleby became keeper of Sand Key Light in 1838. It isn't clear if Rebecca Flaherty was his wife also, but several accounts list Rebecca Flaherty as one of those killed at Sand Key when the lighthouse was destroyed in a hurricane in October 1846.[29,32] Thus ended the long career of the Dry Tortugas' first lighthouse family.

A temporary keeper manned the light until Himinez reported. While the temporary keeper was in charge, the brig ALFRED of Baltimore ran aground on East Key. Although Captain Oliver of the ALFRED assigned no blame to the lighthouse keeper, he did report that he never saw the lighthouse's light. This incident pointed out an important flaw in the design of the lighthouse. The ALFRED had approached from the same direction as the iron door in the lighthouse's lantern. The design, adequate for lighthouses which could not be approached from all directions, created a danger zone for ships approaching the Dry Tortugas.[26] Although the door was apparently replaced soon after, no lamp was placed facing the void until after 1834.[33]

Himinez arrived at the Dry Tortugas at the end of April 1827. He didn't have long to wait for complaints to come in. One month later several shipmasters from New York wrote a letter of complaint. Collector Pinkney was surprised by the complaint as he felt Himinez to be "industrious and temperate, and from the earnest manner with which I have impressed upon him the necessity of giving his utmost attention to the discharge of his duty, believed that he would scarcely venture to neglect it."[34] Himinez responded to the charges saying "(I) am very sorry to find that complaints have been made against me concerning this light. You may rest assured sir, that I keep this light, in perfect order. I trim the lamps three times each night, and in boisterous weather four or five times, if those masters of vessels did not see the light, it is owing probably to fogs or squalls which are very frequent about these Keys."[35]

Himinez resigned his position on July 1, 1828 but later served at other lighthouses in the Florida Keys.[36] He was replaced by Edward Glover, a respectable ship captain who had been wounded on the frigate UNITED STATES during the War of 1812.[37]

By now the condition of the lighthouse was again beginning to deteriorate. When inspected by the Revenue Cutter SOUTH CAROLINA in August 1830, the tower was observed to be a "dirty color between brick and broken plaster". Less than half of the 300 gallons of oil on hand was any good and the roof of the house leaked badly.[38] Additional porches were also requested as their roofs would allow for the collection of more rainwater for storage in cisterns.[39]

Considering the remote location of the Dry Tortugas, it is surprising that it took until 1832 for an assistant keeper's position to be authorized. Before this, a member of the lighthouse keeper's family would be required to tend the light each time the keeper sailed to Key West for supplies. Undoubtedly the stranding of the ship FLORENCE (see page 16) while Glover was away and the light poorly tended highlighted the need for an assistant. Alexander Thompson was the first person named to the position of assistant.[40] Before 1836, Thompson was promoted to head keeper. Elliot Smith was his new assistant.[41]

Audubon Visits the Dry Tortugas

John James Audubon (1785-1851) the self-styled "American woodsman", ornithologist and renowned painter of birds visited the Dry Tortugas in 1832. Famous for his books "Birds of America" (1826) and "Ornithinological Biography" (1831), Audubon was granted use of the Revenue Cutter MARION for two months to conduct collecting expeditions in South Florida. While there, Audubon hoped to collect and observe many new species of birds to add to his portfolio. Audubon's assistant, George Lehman, and a taxidermist from England, Henry Ward traveled with him. The group set out from Charleston, South Carolina in mid-April 1832 on the Cutter MARION.

Audubon

After an uneventful cruise southward, the MARION stopped at Indian Key (50 miles south of Miami) where a local guide named James Eagan joined the party. Led by Eagan, the party successfully collected birds for two weeks. After a short stop at Key West, the MARION sailed on to the Dry Tortugas. Audubon described the Tortugas as consisting of "five or six extremely low, uninhabitable banks, formed of shelly sand, and are resorted to principally by that class of men called wreckers and turtlers." While there, he had a chance to watch turtles laying eggs and he met several wreckers. He had expected wreckers to be like pirates, but instead found them to be well-disciplined and friendly. They took him on several collecting expeditions and presented him with a collection of sea shells on his departure.

Thanks to the help of Eagen, the trip to South Florida was moderately successful. Unfortunately there just wasn't enough time to collect all the birds Audubon wanted. With his two month loan of the cutter just about over, they were forced to return to Charleston on the MARION.

Unfortunately, no mention was made in Audubon's writings about the lighthouse at Garden Key. Audubon was probably staying each night on the MARION, and few rare birds could be expected near the lighthouse.[42]

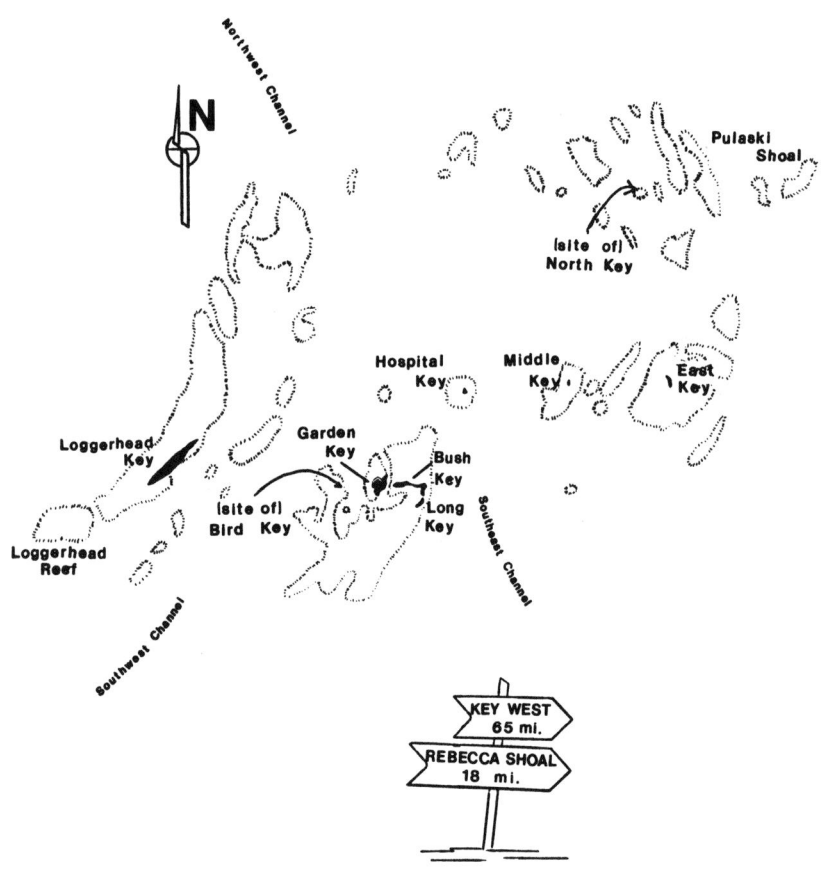

Dangerous reefs extend in all directions from the islands of the Dry Tortugas.

Wreckers at work in the Florida Keys, circa 1865.

The Wreck of the AMERICA

The night of November 6, 1836 was calm and clear off the Dry Tortugas. Just to the east the ship AMERICA, from New York bound for Mobile, Alabama, was making slow progress on a northwest course. Captain Lemuel S. Akin planned to pass east of the Tortugas to shorten the distance of his voyage. Onboard were about 30 passengers, both men and women, most of whom were returning to their jobs after a summer visit up North.

Passenger Charles Nordhoff recorded his experiences on the cruise. With Tortugas light due west, the passengers retired for the night feeling "the joyfulness of the approaching termination of our passage". Just after midnight, a strong shudder awoke the passengers. Up on deck, the crew was frantically backing the sails and taking soundings. Believing the lighthouse on Garden Key had purposely been dimmed to lure his ship to destruction, Captain Akin called out "We are victims of the piratical wreckers!"[3]

The sea was smooth, but the ship was hard aground just off Bird Key. At daybreak, the only wrecker anchored at the Dry Tortugas--the sloop LORETO, went to the aid of the AMERICA.

Lighthouse Keeper or Wrecker?

Because of the protected harbor and the high number of shipwrecks on the surrounding reefs, the Dry Tortugas was a favorite hangout for "wreckers" (the term is used for both the ships and the men engaged in the salvage business in South Florida). In fact, it was relatively rare that one or more wreckers were not on patrol near the islands. Because of the wrecker's presence, it was unusual for lighthouse keepers to be involved in local salvage. One keeper, Edward Glover, aroused more suspicion than most because of his involvement in two wrecks. Was he preventing shipwrecks or causing them? You decide:

On the night of October 2, 1831, the brig CONCORD went aground in bad weather at the Tortugas with a cargo of dry goods and groceries. As no wreckers were in sight, Lighthouse Keeper Glover went to the CONCORD's assistance. With his ship in danger of breaking up, the CONCORD's captain accepted Glover's offer of help. Glover hired the Captain and crew of the sloop SPERMACETTI to assist, and the crew and a part of the cargo were saved. Glover later claimed $15,000 as his salvage fee for the CONCORD. The Wrecking Court allowed him only $750 plus expenses as the judge did not want to encourage lighthouse keepers to engage in the wrecking business.

On November 9, 1831 the ship FLORENCE ran aground on Dry Tortugas' Southwest Reef with a cargo of dry goods and furniture. No light could be seen from the lighthouse until after the ship was aground. Again, the SPERMACETTI came to the rescue, this time with keeper Glover already onboard. Glover told the captain of the FLORENCE that he had been at Key West for the past week, and that his invalid wife and a black woman were tending the light while he was away. Glover also mentioned that the light was too dim, blaming the poor light on his absence. Soon after Glover returned to the lighthouse, the light was seen bright and clear. The FLORENCE was refloated with the assistance of the wreckers and taken to Key West.[3]

"A wrecker of the reef" circa 1865.

The LORETO's Captain Ben Saywer was described as "a stout, burly, red-faced, sun-burned sailor, whose only clothing consisted of a Guernsey shirt, pantaloons rolled up to his knees, and a slouched, weather beaten hat, without stocking or shoes". Suspecting that he could get the AMERICA off the reef without paying the wreckers, Captain Akin refused assistance. Continued efforts to free the ship during the day were unsuccessful. On the morning of the next day, Captain Akin offered the Captain of the LORETO $1,000 if he got the AMERICA off the shoal. This time the LORETO's captain refused as he stood to make much more if the case went to salvage court. Despite jettisoning lead ballast, tobacco and ironware, the ship stayed firmly on the reef.

The next morning, November 9th, the Captain of the LORETO offered the assistance of his sloop and the lighthouse tender, if Captain Akin would let the wrecking court settle the amount of salvage to be paid. This time Akin agreed. "Our wrecker, with his crew of two or three fishermen, among whom the deputy light keeper figured familiarly, had obtained complete possession of his prize", wrote passenger Nordhoff.[32] The wreckers quickly set to work lightering kegs of nails and ironware to Garden Key. The ship came off the reef on the next flood tide, but due to damage to the ship's rudder, the AMERICA only made half the distance to Bird Key. Another gale that night put the AMERICA back on the reef. By morning, the pounding on the reef had mortally injured the ship.

At daybreak of the 10th, passengers and baggage were sent to the lighthouse on Garden Key. Fearing that the AMERICA would break up destroying her remaining cargo, the lighthouse tender was sent to Key West for more help.[3] The tender, guided by the assistant keeper, returned at dusk, either because of a lack of wind or because of concern about the dangers of the passage.[3,32]

Nordhoff reported that during the night, he and Captain Akin overhead Captain Saywer talking to the assistant keeper at the top of the lighthouse. According to his account, the assistant keeper played on his passengers fears of a dangerous voyage to ensure that the crew of the LORETO would be the only ones claiming a share of the salvage. Captain Akin, Nordhoff and "a boy from the lighthouse" sailed to Key West the next day, arriving after a stormy trip in which the boat was almost sunk. Nearly the whole town of Key West turned out at the news (one ship dumped its cargo of oranges into the water to speed their departure) and by November 15th, nine wreckers with nearly 100 men were at work.[3]

Although the hull of the ship was a total loss, the salvage award was for a record $47,471.[32] However, the judge ruled that Captain Sawyer had been remiss in failing to quickly forward news of the wreck to Key West. Captain Sawyer's share was reduced from the usual 50–60 percent to only 35 percent.

In a subsequent interview by the Key West Inquirer, Thompson, the head keeper of the lighthouse, reported that the existing light on Garden Key was inadequate. Due to its distance from the reefs, a mariner could never be sure of his distance from the lighthouse. He recommended two new lighthouses, one at either end of the shoals, be built to replace the Garden Key tower.[32] The Collector of Customs at Key West was in agreement. On November 10th, he had written Washington "Should it not be thought advisable to have all the appropriations made in one year, I would designate as being worthy of attention first the two light houses recommended for the Tortugas in place of the one now there. Many vessels have grounded there during the last year in consequence of the inadequacy of the present light which I have every reason to believe does not arise from any neglect of those in charge."[43] It would be another 20 years before another lighthouse was built at the Dry Tortugas.

A wreck among the breakers, circa 1865.

The lantern of Mobile Point, AL light in 1865. It closely resembles the design of the original Garden Key Light.

Temporary Fixes

It took only 41 days for the Collector of Customs at Key West to drastically change his mind. "Having left it optional with the Keeper of the Tortugas light to resign his office or be suspended under a charge of being habitually intemperate, he has chosen the first, and I would therefore respectfully nominate Mr. Robert R. Fletcher to fill the vacancy ... The light is at present under the charge of a temporary assistant keeper, the regular assistant having resigned his situation on his return from a leave of absence granted to him during the summer."[44] Mr. Fletcher was directed to take charge of the lighthouse as soon as possible. Wrecks continued at about the same pace, but Fletcher received the complete trust of the Collector at least until 1838.

Fletcher was almost replaced in 1837. John W. B. Thompson had been in charge of Cape Florida lighthouse when it was attacked and burned in 1836 by Seminole Indians. Thompson was nearly killed and was stranded on the top of the burnt out tower for two nights. Thompson's only companion, a black man named Aaron Carter, was killed.[45] Because of his notoriety, Thompson gained support in Washington for an appointment. The Key West Collector responded to the pressure by writing back "I cannot form an opinion as to the light in which Mr. Thompson's character and habits were regarded at Washington, but here, where he is well known, they are considered of such a nature as to unfit him for any situation as principal at a lighthouse. At least I should regret having him attached to my District in that capacity."[46] This apparently ended Thompson's attempt. He may have gone on making his living telling the tale of the Indian attack.[45]

Thompson vs the Indians

The attack on Cape Florida lighthouse which earned John W. B. Thompson his notoriety occurred on July 23, 1836 during the Second Seminole Indian War. Cape Florida Lighthouse, located on Key Biscayne near Miami, was then in the midst of a wilderness. Only about 20 families lived in the Miami area in 1836, and most of these had fled because of earlier Indian attacks.

Thompson and another man had been hired in early July 1836 by the keeper, John Dubose, to assist in guarding and tending the lighthouse. On July 18th, Dubose and the other man left for Key West for supplies leaving Thompson and Aaron Carter in charge of the light. Carter was an elderly black man who was probably a slave. Five days later, the Indians attacked.

The Indians, numbering 40 to 50, nearly caught Thompson and Carter before they escaped into the lighthouse. An exchange of musket fire followed, leading to a temporary standoff. After several hours, the Indians set fire to the lighthouse's door. The fire spread to the wooden stairs of the tower, burning fiercely when lamp oil also caught fire. The flames and smoke soon forced the keepers onto the narrow ledge outside the lantern where they were easy targets for the Indian's muskets. Carter was killed and Thompson was shot six times, three times in each foot. Thompson tried to kill himself by throwing a keg of gunpowder into the flaming tower, but the resulting explosion only knocked the stairs down, limiting the extent of the fire. Thinking both keepers were dead, the Indians made an unsuccessful attempt to climb the tower by way of the lightning rod's grounding wire.

Although Thompson received care at the hands of a Doctor in Key West, at least one bullet was never removed. The Indians continued their attacks in South Florida, but the Dry Tortugas was never threatened. The nearest threat was at Key West which was temporarily fortified in 1840 after Indians successfully raided Indian Key (80 miles east of Key West).[45]

While complaints about the Garden Key light continued, studies were made to identify the precise problem. Was it the location of the light, the keeper or the condition of the equipment? Inspectors visited the light and took note of Keeper Fletcher's every action. They found his conduct and actions to be perfectly good, reporting: "We likewise made inquiries of the wreckers (between whom and him no good feelings exist) and they all said that the light is well kept. Fletcher had left Garden Key (at night) only twice and that was to go to Loggerhead Key for wood. The assistant keeper performed all the required jobs while he was gone."

Unfortunately, the diligence of the keeper was offset by the poor condition of the lighting apparatus. Much of the glass in the lantern at the top of the tower was cracked or broken. Several of the panes of glass turned opaque. "I have had panes removed from the lanterns that were actually stained as if painted with various colors." A large smoke vane on the top of iron dome failed to turn in the wind. Smoke from the lamps would blow back into the lantern room, making it hard for the keeper to work and increasing soot on the inside of the windows. The vane could be turned by hand during the day, but it could not be done at night as "there is no way of getting at it save on the outside of the lantern room". All the reflectors, except two, were only thirteen inches in diameter instead of 15. The smaller reflectors were installed in December 1837, but their quality was so bad they were in worse shape than the large ones which had been in use for eight years. The larger reflectors "are easily distinguished at a distance from the others, as they give a much greater light." The lamps "were inferior, and some parts of them nearly burnt through".[47]

A contractor from Boston (Mr. Knowlton) visited the Dry Tortugas lighthouse to make extensive repairs in August 1838. New English plate glass was installed in the lantern along with 23 new lamps with "patent" reflectors. The improvement in the light was so dramatic that it was felt critical to make the same repairs to other lighthouses in South Florida. It was also suggested that the schooner making the annual oil delivery (made in Autumn) be required to stay at each lighthouse one or two hours to allow the keeper to inspect the quality of the oil. Poor oil smoked badly requiring the tube glasses of the lamps to be cleaned frequently. It also was harder to light.[48]

A delivery of tube glasses in 1839 brought about a new problem. The tube glasses and the tin cups that held them were too thin and too small in both height and diameter. The small size caused the glass to heat up and shatter. Because of the new tin cups, the old glass wouldn't fit. An order for 300 new tube glasses was made, but the only supply available was from New York.[49]

In September 1842, Captain Joseph Bethel, the keeper at Dry Tortugas light resigned his position on short notice. Bethel's wife Nicholosa (Mabrity) was the daughter of the Keeper of Key West lighthouse. They also had five children.[36] Bethel and his family probably witnessed the salvage of the schooner NEW YORK. In early May 1842 the ship grounded on Northwest Reef with a cargo of molasses. The ship was gotten off the reef, but she was so unseaworthy that she was taken to Tortugas Harbor for offloading. After everything was removed by the three wreckers present, the pumps were stopped and the ship was allowed to sink in the harbor.[3] Records don't indicate why Bethel resigned, but his replacement was another member of the Thompson clan, Captain John Thompson. Thompson had been a sea captain for nine years.[50]

Only one month after Thompson and his family arrived at Garden Key, a severe hurricane struck the island. Both of Thompson's boats were washed away, the smoke vane on top of the lighthouse was damaged and waves eroded the beach to within 20 feet of the lighthouse tower. The boats were found badly damaged washed ashore on another key.[51] The smoke vane was sent to Key West for repairs and by the end of the year, a contract for $400 was let to build a 100 foot-long wall to protect the lighthouse.[52] The same storm destroyed the dwelling house and kitchen at Sand Key lighthouse. Waves washed through the Key West lighthouse dwelling, but although cracked in two, the structure stood.[53]

One of the constant dangers of living at the Dry Tortugas was making the 70 mile trip to Key West. Generally, the trip was made in small boats given to the lighthouse keepers. In December 1842, a Mr. Beaty was sent to the lighthouse on the 13 ton Revenue cruising boat with a Revenue Service Officer and three men. After they had been gone eight or ten days, word was received from the Tortugas that a very bad storm occurred at the islands at the time they should have arrived. The boat had not been heard from. A schooner was dispatched from Key West to search the surrounding Keys. The schooner returned after an unsuccessful search, but word was soon received that the missing boat was safe. Having missed the Dry Tortugas they had changed course to the northwest and 15 days later reached land off of St. Joseph Bay on the Florida panhandle, over 350 miles away.[54]

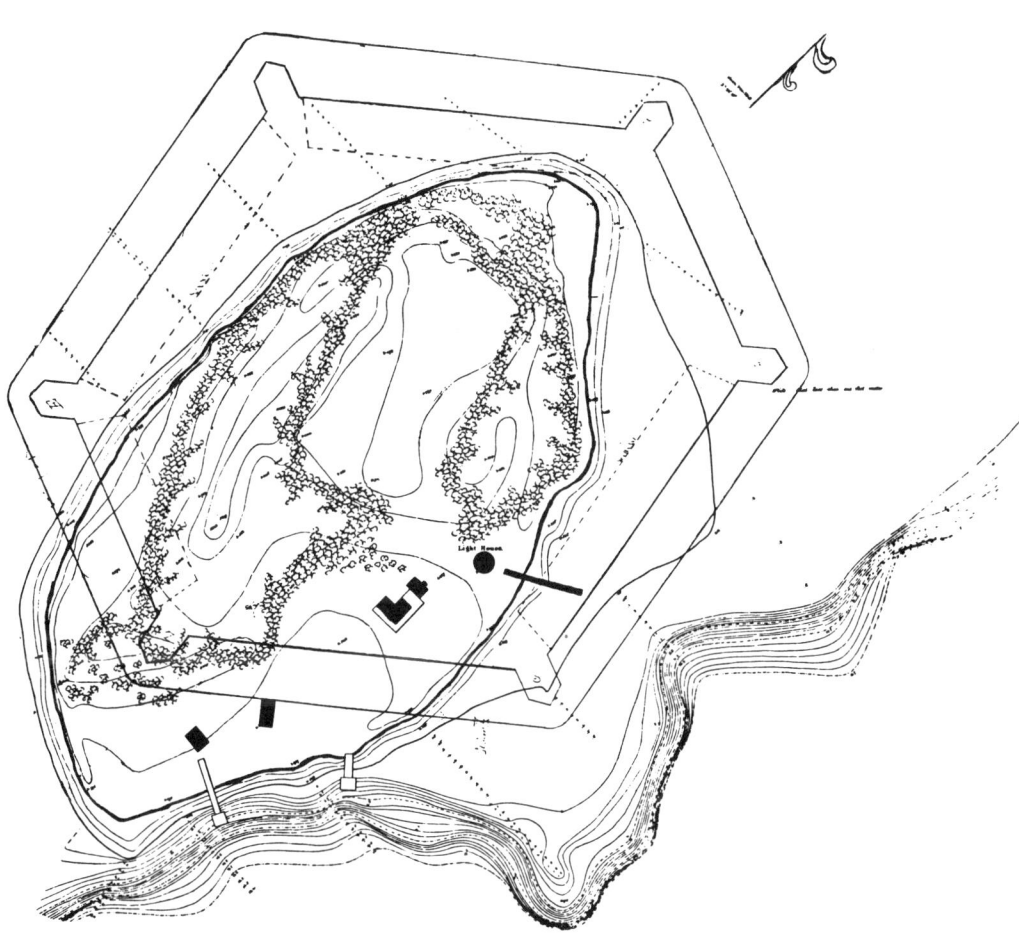

Map of Garden Key, showing proposed location of fort, 1845.

New Neighbors & the Great Escape

Despite Commodore Porter's initial poor recommendation, the thought of the Dry Tortugas as a naval base never died out. When Commodore John Rodgers visited the Dry Tortugas on a return trip from Pensacola in 1829, he was delighted with what he found. Within the reefs were an outer and inner harbor. The outer harbor was safe in all seasons and was large enough for all the navies of Europe to ride at anchor. The inner harbor was deep enough for the largest of warships and had a narrow entrance which could be protected by forts. Despite the disadvantages of no fresh water or firewood, Rodgers reported that no other site was as well situated for controlling the shipping between the Gulf of Mexico, Cuba,

Jamaica and the eastern United States. Additional surveys later the same year found the "greatest abundance" of fish, birds and turtles and a climate "as healthy as the deck of a ship in the same latitude."

Despite these reports, it took increased tensions with Spain (as a result of Texas's independence) and England (the "fifty-four forty or fight" border conflict in Oregon Territory) to swing the mood of Congress towards appropriating money for additional fortifications. Three locations in south Florida were considered critical, Key West, the Dry Tortugas and Key Biscayne (near present-day Miami). Fortified and covered by a proper naval force, these sites would "afford better protection to the commerce of the whole West and Southwest, than ten times the force employed at any other points, or in any other way." For a total cost of four million dollars, the sites would provide the protection of fifty million dollars in military terms. President John Tyler signed an appropriation of $50,000 to start the work in June 1844.[7]

The fort (to be named Fort Jefferson) was designed for about 450 guns in three tiers, making it the largest of all "Third System" style forts in the United States in terms of armament. The barracks of the fort were designed to garrison 1,500 men. The fort would have six sides of unequal length (four sides of 476 feet and two of 325 feet) to match the irregular island shape.[2] From foundation to crown, the eight foot thick walls stand 50 feet tall.[55] Despite 30 years of work, Fort Jefferson was never completed.

The first group of workers to arrive on Garden Key narrowly missed a hurricane. The lighthouse keeper reported that during the hurricane of October 11 and 12, 1846, the surf swept over the entire key except for a small sand ridge on the western end. One of the wharves was wrecked, several small buildings were flattened and all the vessels in the harbor were damaged.[2] Lieutenant Horatio Wright of the U.S. Army Corps of Engineers and a group of workers arrived at Garden Key on December 15, 1846.[56]

Most work on the Fort was conducted in the cool winter months when the danger of malaria and yellow fever was minimal. The workers included skilled masons from the north and slaves hired from the lighthouse keeper and other owners in Key West. The project frequently ran out of money because of small Congressional appropriations, significantly delaying the work.

The slow pace of the work is demonstrated by the fact that temporary buildings for the Fort's work force were still under construction in July 1847. Although the construction crew brought with them a large amount of supplies, they probably used the lighthouse keepers as a handy source of creature comforts. This may have included the lighthouse's kitchen building. The mason's primary duty one month was to build a new chimney for the lighthouse's kitchen.[57]

The harsh living conditions may have contributed to the attempted escape of several slaves from the island in mid 1847. It was first noticed on the morning of Saturday July 9, 1847, when the several boats and schooners that should have been present in the harbor were observed to be gone. Missing were the schooners ACTIVA and VIRGINIA (belonging to the fort), the schooner UNION (belonging to the lighthouse), and Captain Thompson's (the lighthouse keeper) small boat. Only a tiny bateaux belonging to the fort's Doctor remained. A quick alarm and search of the island found the cause.[58,59] Seven of the 11 male slaves on the island, including lighthouse keeper Thompson's slave John were missing.[7] They had taken Captain Thompson's spyglass, a compass, most of their clothing, a small barrel of water and several axes. It was assumed that their goal was to escape to freedom in Cuba or the Bahamas.

By 7 a.m., the men remaining on Garden Key decided to repair the derelict ship VICTOR which was sunk in the harbor and sail to Key West with the news. While the VICTOR was being raised, a lookout in the top of the lighthouse spotted the slaves and their ships 12 miles west of Loggerhead Key. By 8:30 a.m. the VICTOR had been raised and re-caulked enough to be seaworthy. Using hastily made oars, she set out with eight men on board. There was no wind and the water-logged hull of the VICTOR resulted in slow progress. At midday, the run-away slaves sighted the VICTOR. They abandoned the UNION, cutting her masts down, cutting the rigging and unshipping the rudder. Taking to the ACTIVA's boat, they rowed off to southward. The VICTOR couldn't keep up. Having little hope of repairing the faster UNION, with no water and being out of sight of the lighthouse, the chase was abandoned. The VICTOR arrived back at Garden Key at midnight Saturday, just as a strong storm was forming.

The VIRGINIA was later found adrift on the edge of Bird Key shoal. Captain Thompson's small boat was found near the tip of Loggerhead Key, badly damaged. Additional repairs to the

Jack Tier

America's leading author of the mid-1800's chose Garden Key as the site of one of his last novels. James Fenimore Cooper (born 1789, died 1851) was an internationally acclaimed novelist who wrote several classics. He is best known for writing "The Last of the Mohicans". Cooper is also credited with inventing the modern sea novel and with writing the first significant wilderness novels.

Cooper used Garden Key and its lighthouse for the setting of his 1848 novel "Jack Tier". The book was only a modest success and was last printed in 1889. It takes place in 1846 when the United States was at war with Mexico. Stephen Spike, Captain of the brig MOLLY SWASH sails from New York for the Dry Tortugas with a cargo of gunpowder hidden in barrels of flour. Unaware of the true nature of the cargo are the first mate, Harry Mulford and a passenger, the beautiful Rose Budd.

After many close escapes, the MOLLY SWASH is finally boarded by a boat from the U.S.S. POUGHKEEPSIE. All is found in order, but smuggling is suspected because flour is usually shipped north instead of south. Harry and Rose are also suspicious, but they are soon distracted by a mutual romantic attraction. When the MOLLY SWASH arrives at the Tortugas, she anchors near the lighthouse.

Suspicion increases when the lighthouse keeper is missing and Capt. Spike tends the light. The true nature of the voyage is discovered when the keeper is found to be a prisoner on a Mexican ship which arrives for the cargo of gunpowder. A tornado soon strikes, sinking the Mexican ship with all hands, including the light keeper. Through the rest of the novel, Harry and Rose experience various adventures while trying to escape from Capt. Spike. At one point Harry is caught and marooned on a tiny coral rock where it is expected he will soon die.

The climax of the book occurs when Capt Spike's ship surprises Harry while he's standing in front of the lighthouse at night. Harry holds still and the crew becomes convinced he's a ghost. Spike doesn't believe it. He shoots twice at the still frozen Harry but misses. When a mystery shot is fired back at the ship, the crew ducks behind its sides allowing Harry a chance to "disappear".

It is eventually discovered that Jack Tier, a middle-aged cabin boy who has helped Harry and Rose throughout the adventure, is really Molly Swash, Spike's long-lost and spiteful wife in disguise. Capt Spike is finally killed by the crew of the POUGHKEEPSIE and Harry and Rose are rescued. They marry and live "happily ever after" in New York.[60]

Jack Tier's Lighthouse

It is unlikely that the author of "Jack Tier" ever visited the Dry Tortugas himself. His accurate descriptions of the islands and lighthouse were probably based on charts, Coast Pilot descriptions, visits to other lighthouses and interviews of people who had been to the Tortugas. The following passages are from Jack Tier.

"The land proved to be a cluster of low, small islands, part coral, part sand, that might have been eight or ten in number, and the largest of which did not possess a surface of more than a very few acres. Many were the merest islets imaginable, and on one of the largest of the cluster rose a tall, gaunt lighthouse, having the customary dwelling of its keeper at its base."

"In less than five minutes after he had landed, Spike himself was seen in the lantern, in the act of lighting its lamps. In a very short time the place was in a brilliant blaze, reflectors and all the other parts of the machinery of the place performing their duties as regularly as if tended by the usual keeper."

"As they descended and walked through the buildings, Rose also took good heed of the supplies the place afforded. There was flour, and beef, and pork, and many other of the common articles of food, as well as water in a cistern that caught it as it flowed from the roof of the dwelling. Water was also to be found in casks--nothing like a spring or a well existing among these islets."

"As was afterwards ascertained, a family ordinarily dwelt there, but most of it had gone to Key West on a visit, at the moment when the man and boy left in charge had fallen into the hands of the Mexicans, losing their lives in the manner mentioned."

"These good people of the light seem to have lived comfortably, at any rate" (said Harry). Why should they not, maty?" answered Jack, beginning to help to the (turtle) soup. "Living on one of these islets is like living afloat. Every thing is laid in, as for an outward-bound craft; then the reef must always furnish fish and turtle" ... "I've overhauled the lockers pretty thoroughly, and find a plenty of stores to last us a month. Tea, sugar, coffee, bread, pickles, potatoes, onions, and all other knick-knacks."

"Its hardly worth while Don Wan, for you to go into the lighthouse" said Spike. "Tis but a greasy, dirty place at the best, and one's clothes are never the better for dealin' with ile (oil). Here Bill, take the lantern, and get a filled can, that we may go up and trim and fill the lamp, and make a blaze. Bear a hand lads, and I'll be a'ter ye afore you reach the lantern. Be careful with the flame about the ile, for seamen ought never to wish to see a lighthouse destroyed."[60]

VICTOR were made, but heavy winds and seas prevented her departure for Key West. Finally, Thompson and a Mr. Lester reached Key West.

Meanwhile, the Negroes at sea drifted north easterly in the Gulf Stream. After two days at sea they were picked up by a ship near Indian Key (midway between modern day Key West and Miami). They were ordered back into their boat and set adrift. They later came ashore at Indian Key where they were discovered, held and returned to Key West. Jerry Mason (owned by a Mr. Mason) and Jack English (owned by W. F. English) were found to be the ringleaders. "The others were enticed away by their representations" according to Lieutenant Wright. The ringleaders were not allowed back on Garden Key, but the other five were returned before the end of the month.

Lieutenant Wright also wrote "To prevent another attempt on the part of the Negroes to escape and to guard against anything like an insurrection I have deemed it advisable to establish a night watch and have therefore employed Captain Thompson the Light Keeper for that service at $1.00 per night. This would appear to be but a proper precaution when it is considered that it is impossible to ascertain the character and dispositions of the Negroes employed. It has also had the effect of apprising the owners of the security of their slaves so that this will be no difficulty in obtaining as many as may be required in the future. This is an important consideration and would in itself seem to justify the small expenditure necessary to maintain a watch."[58,59]

By 1850, the officer's quarters and the moat wall of the fort were completed. On November 4, 1850, the fort was officially named after Thomas Jefferson. Construction of the main wall of the fort began in 1851.[56]

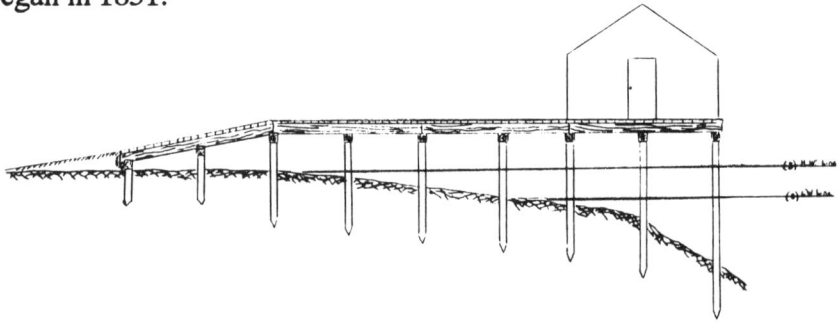

Plan for a proposed wharf and boathouse on Garden Key, 1847.

This photograph, the earliest known of Loggerhead Key, was made about 1900.

A New Light

Despite the improvements that had been made to the lighthouse, everyone recognized the need for some sort of a replacement. The Key West Collector of Customs first made mention of a second lighthouse in 1836. Two years later, he identified Loggerhead Key as the best site. In July 1845, he forwarded the opinions of three experts on the subject. The experts were Captain Day of the Revenue Cutter LEGARE and Captains Dutton and Chase of the Corps of Engineers. Captain Chase was in charge of construction of forts Barrancas, McRea, and Pickens at Pensacola, Florida. The two engineers agreed that Loggerhead Key was the best site and recommended that the lighthouse be 120 feet high. Captain Day felt that the keeper's house on Garden Key should be re-shingled as it leaked badly. All agreed that the present light was "well and neatly kept, and that a hazy atmosphere is the cause of its dimness, as it has sometimes been seen 20 miles."[61]

Meanwhile, ships continued to go aground at the Dry Tortugas. On the night of November 2, 1848, the ship CANTON with a cargo of flour and cotton struck East Key Reef. There were no wreckers in Tortugas harbor at the time, but the fort's dispatch schooner ACTIVA had just unloaded a cargo at the fort. After receiving the permission of the Engineer at the fort, the ACTIVA went to the CANTON's assistance. After part of the 3,290 barrel-cargo of flour had been off-loaded and taken to Garden Key, lighthouse keeper Thompson and his slave John sailed to Key West for more assistance. Thompson's efforts brought 11 more wreckers' ships to the scene. The entire cargo was saved, but the stripped down hulk of the ship was abandoned on the reef. The ACTIVA's claim for salvage was limited by the precedent established in the wreck of the CONCORD. Government vessels would not be encouraged to engage in wrecking.[3]

In Washington, a dramatic change was occurring in the way lighthouses would be administered. Control had been vested in one person, the Fifth Auditor of the Treasury, but in March 1851, Congress directed the Treasury Department to appoint a board of "proper" persons to inquire into the condition of America's lighthouses. Congress also directed that the existing reflector lights be replaced by Fresnel lenses as rapidly as possible. The Fresnel or "classical" lens used reflected and refracted (bent) light to focus light rays into a powerful, narrow, horizontal beam. The "lighthouse board"'s extensive investigations soon resulted in its formal organization into the U.S. Light-House Board. In contrast to its predecessor, the Light-House Board was composed of maritime professionals who knew that money properly invested in lighthouses could save millions in shipping losses.[62]

It was easy for the new Light-House Board to find criticism of Dry Tortugas Light. The 1851 Annual Report of the Coast Survey noted that "Over-estimate of distance, in consequence of dimness of the Tortugas light, is sometimes given as a cause of wreck. Its situation is one of the most important on our whole coast--nearly all the commerce of the Gulf of Mexico passes within sight of it. If additional force be needed to the requirement of a first-class light, it may be found in the military position of the Tortugas. To develop the full usefulness to commerce and the navy, of the extensive fortification now in progress there, as powerful a light as possible seems necessary." The Light-House Board's 1852 report listed projects to improve the Dry Tortugas light as number three in the nation in terms of importance.[63] A ship captain reported the light "very far from perfect ... in fact, two lights are required at this place, one lower than the one now in use, for owing to some local cause, the light is frequently invisible, even with the lighthouse in sight ... On one occasion the writer was becalmed off Tortugas all one night close enough to see the kegs and lower part of the light-house but could not see the light."[64]

When the brig AMESBURY ran aground on Loggerhead Reef in April 1854, the ship's captain was shocked. His estimate put Garden Key light 10 miles away. To make his ship lighter, 170 barrels of molasses that were stored on deck were smashed with axes. The ship remained fast on the reef, and it was only with the help of wreckers that the ship was eventually floated off.[3]

Although considered inadequate, the old lighthouse was still better than nothing. The tower not only survived an August 1856 hurricane, but it also assisted the crew of the government schooner ACTIVA. The storm, running from August 27th to the 28th, was the worst hurricane recorded in the area since 1846. Caught at sea while enroute from Key West, the ACTIVA initially took shelter behind the Marquesas Keys. At 5 p.m. on the 27th, her anchor line broke and she put to sea in an attempt to reach Garden Key. At 3 a.m. the lighthouse on Garden Key was sighted through the gloom. Shortly after, the schooner ran aground on the reef. All of the crew made it safely to Garden Key in the schooner's small boat. Damage on Garden Key was limited to missing slate on the roof of the officer's quarters and water damage to barrels of cement stored on the ground floor of the work buildings.[7]

In 1855, the Lighthouse Board requested a cost estimate for a new lighthouse on Loggerhead Key. The request was sent to the-now-Captain Wright at Fort Jefferson. The request perplexed Wright, as the Board's only requirement was that the tower be 150 feet tall. Wright had no experience with tall towers and had to come up with his own estimates for the upper and lower diameters and the thickness of the walls. He recommended Pensacola or Mobile bricks as they had been found to last longer in the sea air than the cheaper bricks available from New York. He also recommended the use of a steam derrick to hoist bricks up the face of the tower. Two proposals, each for $35,000 were submitted in September 1855 (the cost included $10,000 for a 1st-Order lens).

Based on a recommendation by the Lighthouse Board, Congress appropriated $35,000 "for rebuilding the light-house, on a proper site, at Dry Tortugas and fitting it with a 1st-order apparatus" on August 18, 1856.[65] Captain Wright was transferred from Fort Jefferson (he achieved the rank of Major General in the Union Army during the Civil War and later was the engineer in charge of completing the Washington Monument in Washington, DC[66]) so it was Captain Daniel P. Woodbury who oversaw construction at both Fort Jefferson and the lighthouse.[55]

31

Loggerhead Key is about two-and-a-half miles west of Garden Key.[67] At about one mile in length and 30 acres in area, it is the largest island in the Dry Tortugas.[2] In 1858, the only vegetation of note was a ring of cedar bushes surrounding the island.[68]

Sketch of Mosquito Inlet Light, Florida (now named Ponce de Leon Inlet Light) under construction in 1887. Similar construction techniques were probably used when building the lighthouse on Loggerhead Key.

The Loggerhead Key tower was built on a wooden grillage foundation placed below the water table. By placing the wooden foundation below the water table, it was protected from rats and dry rot. The walls of the tower were built of brick and are approximately 8 feet 9 inches thick with a diameter of the tower of approximately 28 feet. The tower tapers to an exterior diameter of approximately 13 and a half feet. Inside, a central brick column provides support for cut granite stairs. The brickwork is topped by an iron watch room and lantern. Inside the lantern, the 1st-order Fresnel lens stood nearly eight feet high. The lens was purchased from the French firm of L. Sautter and Company of Paris. It was the largest lens then made, and could be seen on an average clear night at a distance of 20 miles. Two galleries at the top of the light provided a lookout and a means to clean the outside of the lantern glass. The tower was left its natural, yellowish red brick color. Other structures were completed nearby: A two story brick structure located near the base of the tower was built for oil storage and the dwelling was located just to the south. The dwelling was also made of a brick, being a two-story structure with Greek Revival features. Each floor had two rooms off a central stair hall. Separate and behind the dwelling, a two-story brick kitchen was built. Brick water cisterns, wash houses and outhouses completed the station. Construction was uneventful and on July 1, 1858, the new lighthouse was completed and first lit. This is the same tower that stands today on Loggerhead Key. The new lighthouse was given the name Dry Tortugas Light, while the lighthouse on Garden Key was renamed Tortugas Harbor Light.[67]

Benjamin H. Kerr was appointed head Keeper and received $600 per year. Kerr was forty-one years old at the time of his appointment, and had previously been keeper at Garden Key since 1850. Charles H. Perry was appointed 1st assistant keeper with John Fritz as the 2nd assistant keeper. Both assistants were paid $300 per year.[36]

As part of the same project which built the Loggerhead Key light, a smaller, 4th-order Fresnel lens (two feet four inches high) replaced the 17 lamps with 21 inch reflectors previously used in the Garden Key tower.[14] The small lens was considered appropriate for a harbor light.[65]

A keeper cleans the lamp in a 4th Order Fresnel lens, undated.

An Increasingly Complex Job

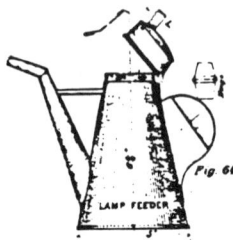

One of the changes implemented by the Light–House Board was the standardization of equipment and tools used at lighthouses. Once all stations were equipped with the same tools, instructions for the operation and maintenance of the lights could be developed. The end result was brighter, more reliable lights, but it also meant that the keepers had to know more and work harder.

One of the Light–House Board's early listings of standard equipment contained over 110 items. Each was carefully sketched and precisely measured. A wide range of items was represented: tools, cleaning supplies, storage boxes and emergency lighting equipment. It varied in complexity from a simple set of scissors (to trim the wicks of lighthouse lamps) to a complete "standard" clock to record the times of sunrise and sunset. Drills, emergency lanterns, leveling devices, measuring cups, and a kit to replace windows broken in storms were also included. [68]

The 1870 instructions for keepers were ten pages long. Lighthouse "keeping" had become quite a science. The first requirement made the change apparent even before the keeper started work: Before entering the lantern room, keepers were required to put on a linen apron to ensure that their buttons wouldn't chip the valuable lens prisims.

For larger lenses, the nighttime duties were performed by two or three keepers, each with a watch four hours in length. The light was lit at sunset so that it would be warmed and at full intensity by twilight. Duties during the night included trimming and adjusting lamp wicks, and ensuring that the lamp and lantern room were properly vented. Keepers were required to stay in the top of the tower so they could instantly respond to any problems with the lamps. Without proper care, excessive soot could be produced or the lamp glass could get too hot and shatter. If the light didn't work right, regulations required that another keeper be awakened to assist with any needed repairs.

Each sunrise when the light was extinguished, an elaborate procedure was followed as the lamps were cleaned and prepared for the following night's operation. Dust, dirt and soot meant that the light wouldn't be seen at as great a distance so great effort was made to ensure everything was spotless. A cover was even placed over the lens after it was cleaned to keep dust from collecting on the lens. [69]

Fort Jefferson circa 1867.

The Fort Becomes a Prison

In the years preceding the Civil War, life continued on quietly with two notable exceptions. One was a minor gold rush of sorts which probably occurred as a result of a find by the keeper of Garden Key, a Mr. Benner. Benner found silver coins worth over a thousand dollars at East Key. One can only imagine the number of holes dug by would be treasure seekers as a result of this discovery![8] The other event occurred in the summer of 1860. The Loggerhead Key lighthouse keeper (Kerr) and one of his daughters showed up at Garden Key with an incredible story. He claimed that his wife, eldest daughter and the assistant keepers had banded together and had attempted to kill him. Kerr held them off with a carving knife until he and another daughter could flee to Fort Jefferson. The sympathetic daughter had been bathing at the time of the incident and arrived at Garden Key nearly naked. What happened later between Kerr and his wife isn't recorded, but both assistants were removed from their jobs.[70]

On the eve of the Civil War, Fort Jefferson was still only half finished.[71] Severe settling of its foundation first became apparent in 1857 when cracks developed in some of the walls. By 1859, some sections of the walls had sunk 12 inches. One of the worst problems was the cracks let seawater into the underground cisterns designed to store water for the ever-thirsty occupants of Garden Key.[56] Only 89 of the proposed 450 cannon were mounted, but

35

the dampness had so rotted their wooden mounts that they were almost useless. In January 1861, Major Arnold with a company of artillery arrived from Boston to make the fort secure for the United States.

Not long after the troops arrived, the Confederate privateer WYANDOTTE came into the harbor. The WYANDOTTE's captain sent a white flag ashore to demand the fort's surrender. One account has Arnold's reply as "Tell your captain I will blow his ship out of the water if he is not gone in ten minutes!" The ploy worked and the fort stayed in Union hands throughout the war. The garrison varied in number from 800 to 1,500 men.[71]

By late 1861, the first contingent of military prisoners arrived at Fort Jefferson. Most were Union soldiers imprisoned for disobeying orders and desertion. As many as 800 prisoners were at Garden Key at one time.[56] The number of prisoners increased dramatically in 1864 when President Lincoln commuted all sentences to hard labor at Fort Jefferson.[72]

Conditions for prisoners varied from harsh torture to benign neglect. One prisoner, named James Dunn, became drunk along with two of his guards when they discovered a supply of whiskey on a ship they were unloading. Dunn was ordered to carry a cannon ball for several hours around the parade ground. Being too drunk to walk, Dunn was strung up by his thumbs. His thumbs swollen to "the size of turnips" he was cut down at sunset and ordered to again carry the ball. A guard was assigned to stick him with a bayonet if he stopped. When Dunn collapsed, the ball fell on his head. The guard prodded him with the bayonet again, trying to get him back on his feet. Dunn's cries prompted the lighthouse keeper to

Two prisoners and a guard at Fort Jefferson.

protest that the "hideous cries" were keeping his family awake. The punishment was continued outside the fort's walls with Dunn being hung by the thumbs and wrists for the rest of the night. Although he lost the use of one arm, it is remarkable that his hands were saved from amputation.

While it may have seemed escape-proof, Fort Jefferson had its security flaws. A shark placed in the moat was generally regarded as harmless. Although rudders and oars of boats at the wharf were supposed to be locked in the guardhouse after dark and the gates of the fort were to be locked each night, guards could be bribed to forget tasks. They also could be bribed to look the other way while transport ships were being unloaded.

The initial goal of the escapees was frequently Loggerhead Key. One escape occurred when a prisoner named Johnny Adare (who was serving a six year term for robbery) paddled on a makeshift raft to Loggerhead Key with a black prisoner. They then stole the lighthouse keeper's boat and rowed to Cuba. Adare was returned by the Cuban government, but the black man stayed free.[71] Harry Blank, condemned for three years at hard labor for larceny and desertion escaped from the post hospital. He paddled to Loggerhead Key on a discarded flight of stairs. Soon after arriving on Loggerhead Key, he was captured hiding in the cactus.[18] One doctor reported that more than 40 other escapes occurred during the short time he was on the island.[71]

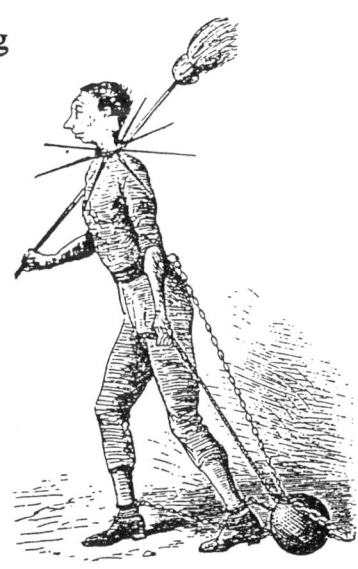

Harry Blank

Loggerhead Key was also the destination of many of the off duty prison guards from the fort. In March 1864, three soldiers were arrested for going to Loggerhead without a pass. A Sergeant's diary recorded a Sunday outing one month later: "Rowley and I went to Loggerhead right away after guard mount and Jim went with us. We took the dog along and he was as sea sick as you please. We got back at one o'clock." In June 1864, the same sergeant went over for an evening party. Several of the men got drunk, one even refusing to return to the fort.[73]

The first major yellow fever epidemic swept through Garden Key in the fall of 1867. It isn't clear if the lighthouse keepers were affected, but with 38 deaths (only two were prisoners) and 270 people sick out of the total of 400 civilians, soldiers and prisoners on the island, fear must have been widespread.[56,74] It was during this epidemic that prisoner Dr. Samuel Mudd volunteered to treat his captors and fellow prisoners. Mudd was in prison for treating John Wilkes Booth after Booth assassinated President Abraham Lincoln. As a result of Mudd's humanitarian work, he was later pardoned and left Fort Jefferson in 1869. During the epidemic, mail bound for Fort Jefferson was hung from a pole erected on Loggerhead Key and picked up by a rowboat as a quarantine measure.[71] Two companies of soldiers were moved to Loggerhead Key to protect them from the sickness. The last case of yellow fever from this outbreak occurred on November 14, 1867.[56]

The Garden Key lighthouse circa 1865. This is the earliest known photograph of the lighthouse and dwelling. The large wind vane on top of the tower looks unchanged from its 1828 contract specifications. The outbuilding with the large fireplace is probably the kitchen.

Hurricanes and Repairs

Over time, heavy rains washed the mortar from between the bricks of the Loggerhead Key lighthouse. By 1868, the mortar on the south and southwest faces of the tower were washed out to a depth of nearly half an inch. A new copper lightning conductor and eight new panes of glass were installed in the lantern, but the oil room and kitchen needed replastering. The yellow fever outbreaks required a rigid quarantine, preventing re-mortaring and other repairs from being made before 1869. It was also recommended that the Loggerhead Key light be painted with alternate black and white bands to make it visible at a greater distance.

In 1870 minor repairs were made to both towers. At Loggerhead, a new boat house was built while at Garden Key repairs were made to the lantern, keeper's dwelling and outbuildings. The lighthouse on Loggerhead Key was first painted around 1870.[65] Its brickwork had previously been a natural yellow-red brick color while the iron lantern was painted black. Although the black paint tended to make things very hot in the tropical environment, it was the typical color for lanterns because it minimized reflections which could confuse mariners. The new color scheme for the brickwork was the upper half black and the lower half white. In addition to being distinctive (the nearest similar colored lighthouse is the iron skeleton lighthouse at Hillsboro Inlet Florida) this color scheme provides good contrast to the area's billowy white clouds and low green foliage.[75]

In August 1873, a second major outbreak of yellow fever occurred on Garden Key. The fever was brought in by the 13-year-old son of the Assistant Surgeon who caught the disease in Key West. On

September 6, 1873 all healthy soldiers from Fort Jefferson were evacuated to Loggerhead Key. Only about 30 people (civilians, two doctors, soldiers acting as nurses and the lighthouse keeper) stayed behind on Garden Key with the sick.[2] In all, 24 people came down with yellow fever, of which 12 or 13 died.[56]

A hurricane hit the Dry Tortugas in October 1873 while the sick were still recovering. The storm damaged both lighthouses and the dwelling of the Garden Key light.[7,67] As a result of the yellow fever epidemics and hurricane damage, Fort Jefferson was abandoned by the Army in 1874.[75] On Loggerhead Key, the metal top of the lighthouse vibrated so strongly in the hurricane force winds that the metal anchors which held it to the brickwork came loose. The damage was so bad that the tower was considered unsafe. It was recommended that the entire tower be rebuilt, at an estimated cost of $150,000. Congress appropriated $75,000 on March 3, 1875 to begin work.

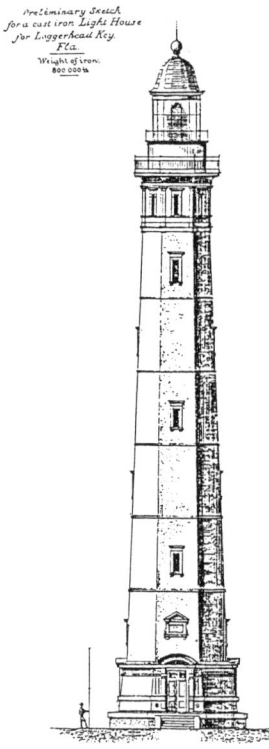

The iron replacement tower for Loggerhead Key 1876.

The light on Loggerhead Key being considered essential, repairs were made to keep the damaged tower operational until a new one could be built. Just below the iron lantern, narrow nine-foot-long vertical sections of the brick work were removed and replaced one at a time. The anchors holding the iron lantern to the brick section were extended farther down into the bricks. Reports stated "When it is remembered that the tower is about 150 feet high, the difficulty in making these repairs will be better appreciated." The repairs were completed in 1875.[65]

Back on Garden Key, the lighthouse tower was also under scrutiny. In March 1874 the Lighthouse Board noted that the old tower was obstructing the parade ground and "greatly injuring the appearance of the interior of the defensive works." The Board proposed that a new lighthouse be built on the walls of the fort. Benefiting from the height of the walls, a new light would consist simply of a watchroom surmounted by a lantern.

A feasibility study found that the nearby stairway of bastion C could be modified to provide a foundation for the lighthouse without hindering its use by troops. After receiving authorization by the War Department, the project was funded by a Congressional appropriation for $5,000 in March 1875. The design of the 1864 Fort Point lighthouse built in a similar situation on the walls of Fort Winfield Scott, California (both the fort and the lighthouse still stand underneath the Golden Gate Bridge) was consulted, but not adopted.[7,76] A wrought iron tower was considered necessary because a brick structure on the wall of the fort would create dangerous fragments if hit by exploding shells.[7]

Before any new work could begin, another hurricane roared across the Dry Tortugas in September 1875. Doors and windows throughout the Loggerhead Key station were badly damaged. Water gutters were knocked down and the lightning rod on the top of the tower was damaged. The keepers reported new damage to the masonry caused by vibrations of the lantern during the high winds. On Garden Key, the old tower was declared almost useless and efforts were sped up to ensure its quick replacement.

The new Garden Key light would be a hexagonal tower of boiler-plate iron, having a balcony and cylindrical parapet. The iron was ordered November 26, 1875. On site construction of the tower was begun in February 1876. The lens from the old tower was moved to the new one and first lit on April 5, 1876.[65] The new tower was probably painted a dark brown.[77]

The "new" iron lighthouse on Garden Key, circa 1880.

41

Neighboring Lights

With the lighting of the lighthouse on Loggerhead Key in 1859, attention could be turned to other areas of the Florida Reefs which still posed a threat to mariners. Rebecca Shoal, 18 miles east of Garden Key, was one such area of concern. Marking the eastern side of a wide north-south channel, Rebecca Shoal was probably named after a shipwreck occurring there in 1816.[78] As if Rebecca's 12 foot deep shoals weren't enough, just east was an area of even shallower shifting sand banks which soon came to be known as "the quicksands".

Rebecca Shoal

The first effort to mark Rebecca Shoal was made in 1854. Each annual attempt failed as storms quickly destroyed everything as soon as it was built. Work on a beacon was finally abandoned in 1858. This was the only notable failure for the district engineer, LT George Meade, who, within five years, would be commanding the Union Army at the Civil War Battle of Gettysburg. An unlighted buoy was placed to mark the shoal in 1858. In 1873, a single pile beacon was tried again, but it lasted only six months before it was destroyed in a storm. A 75-foot tall iron beacon marked the shoal from 1879 until 1886. It took three years to build and cost nearly $40,000. It was torn down and replaced by a wooden lighthouse on iron piles. First lit on November 1, 1886, the lighthouse contained a 4th order lens and was manned by a keeper and two assistants.[79] Rebecca Shoal Light was converted to automatic operation and unmanned in 1926. The old foundation piles supported a light until 1985, when they were replaced by a modern skeleton-tower structure.

Another light was erected at the eastern tip of the Dry Tortugas on Pulaski Shoal in 1936. Never manned, the light showed a flashing white light produced by a 500 mm glass lens. The light was fueled by acetylene gas. It was 49 feet above water. A similar tower was built at the same time on Tennessee Reef in the middle Keys.[80] In 1986, nine lighted buoys and eight unlighted buoys were placed around the Dry Tortugas to mark the administrative boundaries of the National Monument. Together with several other local lighted and unlighted aids to navigation, and the lighthouse and radiobeacon on Loggerhead Key, the Dry Tortugas is no longer a dangerous obstacle to mariners.

Tennessee Reef

Garden Key Lighthouse in 1897.

Quiet Times Despite War

Despite the report of additional damage to the Loggerhead Key light in the hurricane of 1875, all new work was put off until an engineer could observe the vibrations of the tower in high winds. Apparently, additional minor repairs corrected the problem as no further mention was made of it in later reports.

Things were also quiet on Garden Key. The old brick lighthouse tower was taken down in 1877, and a wooden partition was placed across the stairway inside the new tower to prevent excessive winds. Both stations were considered to be in good condition after minor repairs and painting in the late 1870's.[65]

There was an overall lull in the number of shipwrecks in the Dry Tortugas during the 1870's, but some ships still came on shore. One was the Dutch bark AURORA in February 1879. No blame was attached to the lighthouses as the AURORA stranded during a fog. On the morning of September 14, 1880 the American bark CARIBOU was sighted in distress by the keeper of Loggerhead Key Light twelve miles to the west. The ship was sailing with "short sails" and her flag upside down. Investigating in the lighthouse's small boat, the keeper and his assistant found that the captain and crew of ten had been stricken with fevers. Two sailors and the captain had died and been buried at sea. Assisted by the first mate, who was the only one up and about, the keepers made sail and took the ship into Tortugas Harbor. From there, seven men from a pilot boat sailed the ship to Key West where the CARIBOU's crew was hospitalized. All eventually recovered.

During a strong gale in September 1882, a boat with four crewmen aboard from the schooner WILLIAM S. FARWELL was swept out to sea while trying to make Loggerhead. The FARWELL had struck a section of Dry Tortugas' Southwest Reef called Miller Rock. The Captain had gotten the ship off the reef and anchored, but the heavy swells threatened to sink the damaged ship. The small boat was dispatched to Loggerhead Key light to get assistance, but the boat was blown to sea and feared lost. Fortunately, after two nights and three days at sea, the boat was picked up by a passing ship. All four men were safe. After temporary repairs at Tortugas Harbor, the FARWELL went on to Key West.[3]

The 1880's were also comparatively quiet times for the lighthouses in the Dry Tortugas. On Loggerhead Key, a new boathouse was built in 1880 on the western shore. Mineral-oil lamps were installed in 1884 and in 1899 two new wash-houses were built. On Garden Key, the official name of the lighthouse was changed in 1883 from Dry Tortugas Harbor light to Tortugas Harbor Light. The keeper's house on the parade ground was replaced in 1888.[65] The same year, Loggerhead, Garden and Bird Keys were reserved as a national quarantine station with the first patients arriving in April 1889 with smallpox. Disinfecting and fumigating equipment were set up on Garden Key.[56]

The "new" keeper's dwelling on Garden Key circa 1890.

A buoy depot for the storage and repair of navigational buoys was also established on Garden Key in 1889. The depot included a wharf, an outside storage area, a buoy shed and a blacksmith shop. The buoy shed was used to scrape, repair and paint buoys while parts were fabricated in the blacksmith shop. Buoys were loaded on and off ships at the wharf. The wharf wasn't maintained very well and in an 1893 gale it was washed away. The Lighthouse Board later reported "During the quarantine season, from May to November, it is not advisable to visit or communicate with this depot, as the light-house tender would thereby be made liable to quarantine by the Florida State Health Board at all the ports of Florida."[81]

A buoyant new era in history began in 1890 as America became the "can-do" nation. It was the age of progress and invention.[82] This same spirit prevailed within the Lighthouse Board. At the Dry Tortugas this spirit was first manifested by the addition of red sectors to both of the lighthouses on April 30, 1893. The light on Loggerhead Key had one red sector while the Garden Key light had three. The change was accomplished by attaching large sheets of red glass to the inside of the lantern. The red areas were placed facing particularly dangerous sections of the reefs. If the captain saw red, he knew not to head towards the light.[65]

The system of lights still wasn't perfect for in October the Captain of the British Bark CARMALITA COMPOSITE claimed he mistook the Loggerhead Light for Tortugas (Garden Key) Light. His ship stranded on Bird Key before he realized the error. A storm blew through, and although the crew safely made it to Fort Jefferson, the CARMALITA COMPOSITE was a total loss.[3]

The year 1893 also saw renewed interest in the Dry Tortugas by the War Department. Ordering the quarantine station removed, the Department stated "The Dry Tortugas is too valuable a military station to be surrendered for any other purpose." Some sort of compromise was worked out since the quarantine station continued operation until 1900.

With increasing calls for the United States to intervene in Cuba's revolution from Spain, the Dry Tortugas had regained its strategic importance. Spain had a powerful, if somewhat outdated fleet. If the United States went to war with Spain over Cuba, our coasts could be attacked. The waters near the Dry Tortugas had been used as the traditional winter drill grounds for the U.S. Navy's powerful North Atlantic Squadron. To avoid provoking Spain, the exercises were suspended for two years, but in 1898 they were scheduled again. On January 24, 1898, the battleship U.S.S. MAINE left the other ships of the American fleet at anchor in the Dry Tortugas. She sailed for Havana, Cuba to show the flag and to protect American citizens in the event of violence. Only a few weeks later, while at Havana, the MAINE suffered a tremendous explosion in the forward part of the ship. Out of 350 officers and men onboard, 260 died in the blast. The disaster was blamed on a Spanish mine, and led to the war cry "Remember the Maine!". War was declared against Spain on April 21, 1898.[83]

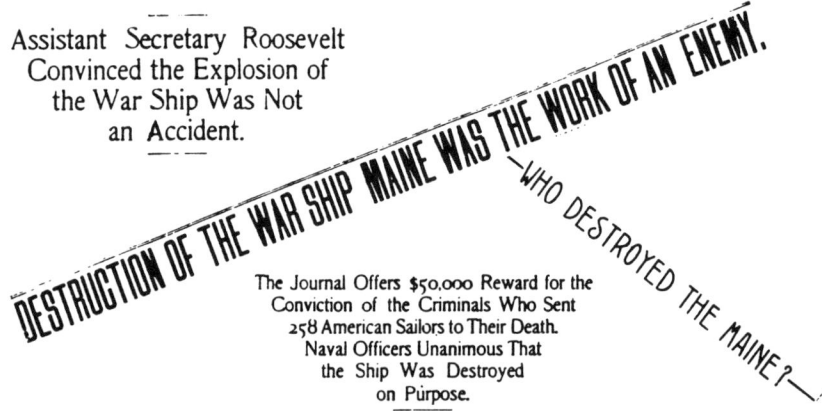

A panel headed by Rear Admiral Hyman G. Rickover in 1976 reached the conclusion that the cause of the explosion was internal. Its most likely source was a spontaneous combustion fire in the coal bunker adjacent to a powder magazine. Coal fires of this type are a gradual process, so it is possible that the fire which sank the U.S.S. MAINE began while the ship was at the Dry Tortugas.[84]

Fort Jefferson was again garrisoned by Army troops. The Navy also began construction of new wharfs and two coal sheds just outside the fort. Perhaps due in part to the rapid preparations, the war with Spain was quickly over. A peace treaty was signed in December 1898.

The Navy continued to have a strong presence in the Dry Tortugas after the War. In 1900, the military reservation of Fort Jefferson and the buoy depot facilities were transferred over to the Navy Department. The Army garrison was replaced by a 29-man Marine Corps garrison in 1901, at about the same time as the red sectors were removed from Garden Key lighthouse.[85] The coal sheds were in use until 1908.[56]

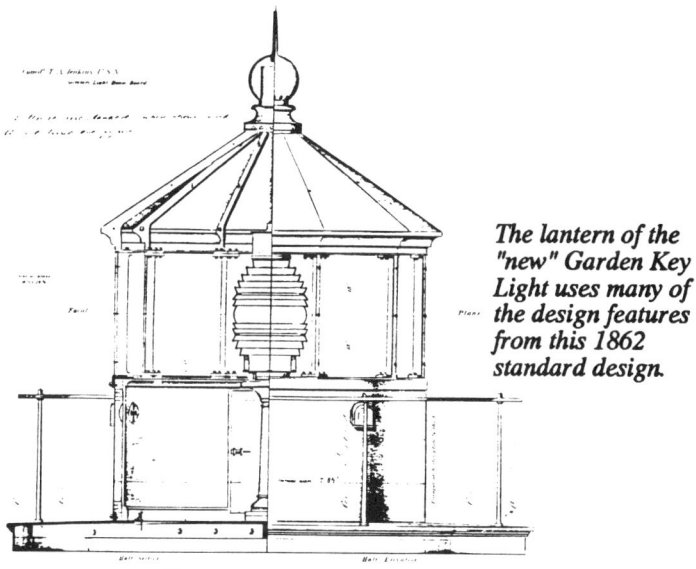

The lantern of the "new" Garden Key Light uses many of the design features from this 1862 standard design.

The End of an Era

The new century began with a change to lighthouse administration, new neighbors and improvements to the station on Loggerhead Key. In 1903, the Lighthouse Board was moved from the Department of Treasury to the Department of Commerce.[86] The next year, a section of land on the north end of the island was granted to the Carnegie Institute of Washington DC for construction of a marine laboratory. In 1906, two storerooms and new porches were added to the lighthouse station.[65] In 1910, the Lighthouse Board was replaced by the Bureau of Lighthouses, which still operated under the Department of Commerce.[86]

On October 17, 1910, a great hurricane passed over the Tortugas. This record storm started at 8:00 a.m. with a wind from the east. The wind increased and shifted to the north until the eye of the storm passed over the islands at about 2:15 p.m. After a calm of about 15 minutes the wind returned, this time from the southwest. It wasn't until nightfall that the winds finally died down. At the Loggerhead lighthouse, the barometer went to a low of 27.96 and the wind was estimated at 100 miles per hour.[87] Several of the glass lantern panes were blown out and the lighthouse wharf was badly damaged.[88] A high sand ridge formed on the beaches, even higher than the ones formed in the hurricanes of 1846 and 1875. As testimony to the strength of the storm, bits of seaweed were found lodged in the lamps at the top of the tower, 160 feet above sea level. The marine lab was also badly damaged with a dormitory destroyed, the roof of the main building blown 500 feet

Carnegie Institution of Washington
Marine Biological Laboratory at Tortugas, Florida

The new century began on Loggerhead Key with a grant of land on the north end of the island to the Carnegie Institution of Washington DC. The "Carnegie Lab" was established in July 1904 "for the study of marine life of the tropical Atlantic". It was originally designed as a temporary station with portable buildings to support several investigators at a time, but the lab lasted nearly 40 years.[65]

The lab consisted of a main laboratory building and sleeping porch, a detached lab, a kitchen, a windmill for pumping salt water and air to aquariums, a dock, a shipways, two small outhouses and a cistern. The labs and outhouses were built in New York and shipped to Loggerhead for assembly, while the rest of the buildings were built on site. About 50 palm trees were planted around the lab to shade the buildings and provide hurricane protection. All the buildings, chemicals, lab glassware, and furniture cost only $4,800. The lab's research vessel was a 57-foot-long ketch, with a 20 horsepower auxiliary engine.[87]

One immediate effect of the lab may have been the 1908 declaration of the Dry Tortugas as a wildlife refuge to protect the sooty tern. These birds, laying their eggs directly on the sand, were almost wiped out by egg collectors. The "eggers" took eggs for the breakfast tables of Key West.[55] *Nature also took its toll of the birds. A thunderstorm on April 14, 1909 resulted in the deaths of thousands of migratoy birds. The keepers reported "They covered the ground like a multicolored blanket ... the lighthouse had been newly painted, and in the morning it was literally plastered with brilliant feathers."*[87] *It is not clear if all the birds died from flying into the lighthouse or if the force of the wind killed them.*

The lab was only open during the summer because of high insurance rates for shipping during the hurricane season. In addition to the scientists, a crew of part timers consisting of two sailors, an engineer, a steward, a lab servant and a "man of all work" stayed at the lab. Transportation to and from the island was originally provided by the Navy as part of their operation of the Fort Jefferson coal station. When the coal station closed down in early 1909, a new lab vessel was built at a cost of $25,000. The new ship, the ANTON DOHRN, was a 70-foot steamer. Besides being used for research and transporting lab personnel, the DOHRN also provided transportation for lighthouse families, their furniture and food supplies.[87]

The ANTON DOHRN

In return for their transportation, the lighthouse keepers watched the lab and assisted the scientists with their studies. Several of the studies amused the keepers, including an experiment to cross breed two types of land snails. One of the keepers was later quoted as saying "Once they got one live cross-bred baby snail; an' my dear man, wasn't they tickled, though? They go down in divin' suits on the reef, to see what's down there--as if who cared! They paints diff'rent kinds o'sardines, too, an' feeds 'em to the fishes to see which kind they like best. They says snappers is the most educated kind o' fish there is. But if that ain't waistin' money, to find out about fishes' education, what is?"[89] Another study required the keepers to preserve in alcohol birds killed by striking the light tower. During a five month period, 21 birds from 14 different species were collected.[87]

The lab is best remembered for its pioneer work on coral reef and mangrove communities in the western hemisphere and as the site of both the first underwater black and white photographs and the first underwater color photographs.

The Carnegie lab survived several hurricanes, a temporary closure due to the First World War, reduced financing during the depression and several recommendations to relocate it because of its isolation. The final years were busy, with 12 to 18 scientists at work, but in 1939, financial considerations and the shift from macro to micro biology resulted in its closure. Thirty-five volumes of research were published by the Tortugas Lab, the last in 1942.[87]

to the south and the entire machine shop moved five feet from its foundations. It was reported that nearly every leaf of every plant was torn to shreds. On Garden Key, the lighthouse was put out of operation for a week and the barracks roof damaged. Fortunately, there were no reports of personal injury.[88] Given the damage to the top of the tower, it is not surprising that the old 1st order lens was replaced at about the same time. Constructed by the Paris, France firm of Henry Lepaute, the new lens (numbered USLH 213) was a 2nd order bivalve or "clam shell" lens. Shaped like the two halves of a giant clam's shell, the lens rotated to produce a flashing light. The lens' rotation was powered by a clockworks which held gears and an eight-inch diameter cable drum. One end of 1/4-inch steel wire cable was attached to the drum and the other to a weight (of 60 or more pounds). The weight moved down the

The 2nd-order lens formerly used on Loggerhead Key.

hollow center pillar of the lighthouse (this pillar also supports the inside end of each step). The clockworks used gears to convert the energy of the falling weight to power a constant rotation of the gears. The heavy lens and its turntable sat in an iron trough filled with mercury. Being very dense, a 10-inch deep pool of mercury was sufficient to float the lens. There was so little friction that the lens could be turned with one finger. The clock needed to be wound only once every 16 hours, but it was probably wound each morning when the light was extinguished. With the lens rotating once every 40 seconds, ships passing the Dry Tortugas would see one white flash every 20 seconds.[90]

An even stronger hurricane smashed into the islands on September 10, 1919. The barometer plunged to 27.57, the lowest yet recorded at the Tortugas. The marine lab again suffered as its wharf, the two main lab buildings and the machine shop were seriously damaged. Wire cages for a snail breeding experiment were blown or washed away.[87] Waves washed across Loggerhead Key and the wind was estimated to be blowing at 135 miles per hour. The keepers later bragged that the lighthouse bent over five feet in the storm, that 14 lantern panes were broken and that the lens rotated so quickly that the mercury spilled out. The keeper was only able to stop it and prevent damage to the gears by clogging it with ropes. The keepers also stated that after the storm, the island was covered with fish scales "blowed clean off the fishes in the ocean an' scattered everywhere".[89] On Garden Key, the fort's moat was breached and the steel girders of the coal sheds were twisted and mangled.

One disaster was followed by another. The night of January 4–5, 1912 was much like any other at the nearly abandoned Fort Jefferson. At midnight, the lighthouse keeper used the outhouse adjacent to his dwelling on the parade ground. At 2:30 a.m., the

The soldier's barracks shortly before it burned down. The keeper's outhouse may be the small white building to the left of the lighthouse's dwelling.

outhouse was discovered to be on fire. From the first it was beyond control. It soon spread to an adjacent shed, and then to the dwelling itself. There was no fire-fighting gear at the fort, and despite being on an island, water was not readily accessible. Little could be done to fight the fire. A strong wind from the northwest spread the now raging fire to grass and brush on the top of the fort's walls. Cinders blew through the sally port catching the bridge over the moat on fire.

Eddies of wind carried more cinders onto the roof of the Marine barracks (formerly known as the soldier's barracks). The roof of this building would normally be covered with a layer of fireproof tin, but the October 1910 hurricane had torn most of this protective covering off, leaving sections of dry, sun baked wood. With the fort nearly abandoned, no repairs had been made. At 4:30 a.m., the first flames were noticed from the roof of the barracks.

Efforts to put out this new fire were made, but they too were unsuccessful. The fire advanced through the attic of the barracks until at 3:30 p.m. the next afternoon it burst through the roofs of the three south sections. At 10:30 p.m. the roof fell in and to some extent smothered the flames. Kitchens behind the barracks and a latrine were also destroyed. Only the bridge over the moat was saved. Because of its brick construction, it was believed that the barracks could be repaired for half of its original cost.

Outhouses and kitchens behind the barracks were also destroyed in the fire.

No definite cause of the fire could be determined, but it was believed that either the keeper or a member of his family had left a candle or a cigarette burning in the outhouse.[7] The keeper's house was never replaced as the next year the lighthouse was automated and its characteristic changed to one white flash every two seconds.[91] The light on Garden Key was considered unnecessary and discontinued in 1921.[92]

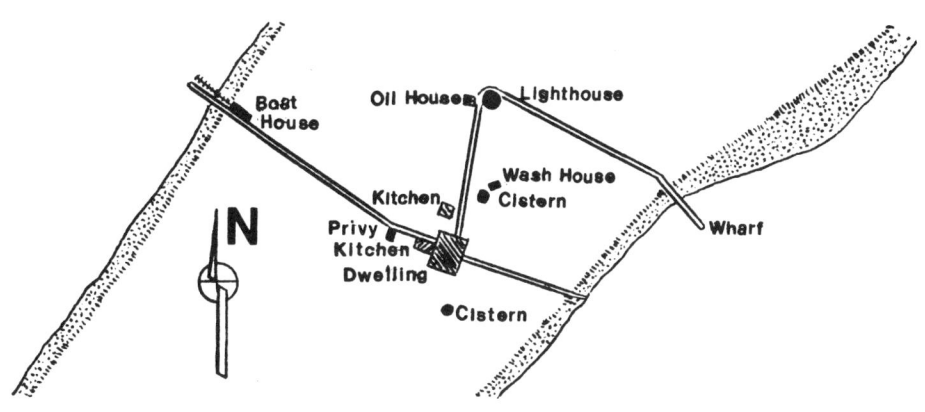

Map of Loggerhead Key Light Station in 1904.

Flashing Lights

A major renovation was made to the buildings at Loggerhead Key in 1922 and 1923. A new oil storage building was constructed near the base of the lighthouse while the original oil house was converted to house equipment for a radiobeacon. The conversion included a roofed passage to connect the radio room to the lighthouse. A new residence (a one-story bungalow style) was built for the head keeper to the north of the tower. It had running water and a bath tub.[67,93] The old kitchen was also converted into living quarters.[67] The cost of the renovation was $6,500.[65]

A problem with the 2nd order lens was fixed in 1923. The rotating lens reflected light off the interior of the lantern causing secondary flashes which could confuse ships at sea. Sixteen radial curtains were initially installed, but the final and most effective repair was to the lens itself. End screens were installed around the edge of the lens and thin vertical copper screens were placed on the center lines of the lens panels. The screens turned with the lens, did not reduce the intensity of the flash and reduced secondary flashes. The fix used at the Dry Tortugas was recommended for other bivalve lenses.[94]

Logbooks from the Loggerhead Key lighthouse are on file in the National Archives for the period 1925 to 1940. The logs record each day's weather and the work accomplished at the station. Most of the work recorded involved cleanup of the grounds and painting. Coast Guard boats frequently visited the station asking for information or water. In April 1926 a Coast Guard boat assisted the keeper and third assistant when the lighthouse's tender (Number 31) rudder got jammed and the boat grounded on a shoal. Later the same year, lightning struck the lighthouse tower breaking eight panes of glass. The damage was repaired the next day. In 1927 the log reads "Keeper Hall went to assist work party (ed. from a visiting tender) and got his head broke by falling water bucket". Only one visit to the laboratory was recorded when in 1928 the "Carnegie Doctor had the light over". In January 1933 a Coast Guard boat came to the station asking about some Spanish fishermen who were at Fort Jefferson. The log records "(The fishermen) said I gave him permission to go in there, I would be foolish to do that."[93] In 1935 the Dry Tortugas, including Loggerhead Key, were made part of Fort Jefferson National Monument, managed by the National Park Service.[67]

An underwater cable had linked Fort Jefferson with Key West in 1899, and two way radio sets were in use at the fort in 1904 and 1917, but the first mention of a radio on Loggerhead wasn't until 1926.[56,93] Radio had proven very valuable in the operation of the Lighthouse Service, not only in providing communications relating to approaching storms, supplies and operations, but also as an aid to navigation through the use of the radio compass and radio-beacons to guide ships. Radios also offered the benefit of lessening the loneliness of life at lighthouse stations.[95]

Loggerhead Key in 1928 looking northwest.

The new keeper's dwelling on Loggerhead Key in 1926.

Compassionate private citizens began donating commercial radio receivers to lighthouse keepers in the early 1920's. In 1926, then Secretary of Commerce Herbert Hoover learned that many light stations still did not have a radio. With no federal funds available, he made an appeal to the press he saying: "I don't know of any other class of shut-ins who are more entitled to such aid. The Government does not pay them any too well, and the instruments which they can hardly afford are in many cases their only means of keeping in touch with the world." The appeal resulted in the donation of more than 300 radio receiving sets, giving nearly all the isolated lighthouses a set by 1929.

The radios opened a whole new world for the keepers. A letter from Alligator Reef Light in Florida was typical: before receiving the radio, "When a President was elected sometimes it has been one month before we knew who was elected: this time, when Secretary Hoover was elected and it was announced to the world, we heard it as soon as anybody else. The last two big fights when it was announced who was champion we heard it. We listen also to ministers preaching, and there is singing; it is almost the same as being in church."[95]

A marine radiobeacon, powered by generators, was installed in 1928 on Loggerhead Key. The radiobeacon, which transmitted groups of three dashes on 286 kilocycles, was used by ships to obtain navigational fixes beyond the reach of the light and in bad weather.[96]

It wasn't until 1933 that the light itself was electrified. With electric light bulbs, the lens produced a light equal to 1.5 million candles.[96] The light's advertised range remained at 19 miles, but that was because its geographic range (limited by the height of the lighthouse tower and the curvature of the earth), while the light's visual range was calculated at 27 miles.[97] Under unusual conditions, the light could be seen at a much longer distance. On the night of September 22, 1933, the SS JOSEPH R. PARROTT was leaving Key West for Mobile Alabama. At 11:10 p.m. on a clear, starry night, with no clouds, the PARROTT saw the light as "a half disk or circle, sweeping from west to east. This disk was very clear, with no glare effect, and showed as much light a light as you can imagine, without seeing the actual light. Outside the disk, the glare extended for some distance." The light was plotted and found to be 53.6 miles from the ship. One day short of a year later, the MS SUN saw the loom of the light when approximately 52 miles northwest of the station. The SUN's captain reported, "The atmospheric conditions were apparently very clear, following a squall. The ship's officer reports a striking display of continuous lighting to the northwest from the light station, in a towering bank of clouds beginning at sunset and culminating in the squall passing to the eastward." Similar occurrences of unusual visibility range are common, but only in the far north.[98]

A typical lighthouse generator plant, in 1941.

Communications with the lightstation were improving, but making the trip from the lighthouse to Key West in the station's small motor boat was still a dangerous proposition. In 1938, experiments were made with carrier pigeons. A Lighthouse Service bulletin noted: "In tending a great many of the minor automatic lights, small boats, often with only one or two men aboard, have to spend long periods of time in regions entirely devoid of population. By carrying homing pigeons, it is expected that some of the anxiety of such work will be removed. Consideration is also being given to the carrying of pigeons aboard the small boat in which the keepers and their families at Dry Tortugas Light Station travel to and from Key West, a distance of 65 miles over a route which lies nearly 100 miles from the mainland."[99]

On the eve of World War II, the Lighthouse Service was transferred to the U.S. Coast Guard. Few changes were immediately apparent at the lighthouse, as most of the civilian keepers were enlisted into the Guard, most as Chief Petty Officers. When the war started in late 1941, elaborate plans were made to "blackout" navigational aids as a means of hindering enemy air raids. As it turned out, the main threat to the U.S. coast was from submarines. Starting in Mid-February 1942, Nazi U-boats sank 24 ships in the Florida Straits. From these ships many were killed, but 504 men were saved. A major concern was that the lights from lighthouses would silhouette ships and aid enemy submarine operations. The lighthouses couldn't be turned off, as this would result in many more casualties from groundings, so a wartime "dimout" was tried.[100] On May 8, 1942, all of the lighthouses along the Florida Straits were ordered to reduce the intensity of their lights. Dry Tortugas light went from 1,500,000 to 5,000 candela.[101]

Loggerhead Key was probably one of the many lighthouses that had extra personnel assigned during the war to act as coastal lookouts. Starting shortly after the outbreak of the war, the lookout's duty was to watch for enemy submarines, ships or planes. Besides a radio and a pair of binoculars, their only equipment was a simple sighting instrument called a pelorus that was used to determine the bearing of an object. The lookouts were probably posted outside of the tower on the gallery (the balcony just below the glass windows of the lighthouse's lantern). This location would provide the best view while avoiding the lens's blinding light. The men probably slept on extra bunks in the main dwelling.

Better communications and knowledge of weather provided advance warning of a hurricane in 1944. While the storm was still over Cuba, the lightstation crew at Dry Tortugas was ordered to move into the lighthouse with several days of provisions.[102] The warnings were well founded, as on October 18, 1944 the center of the storm passed directly over the islands. Wind gusts of 120 miles per hour were recorded, but no reports of damage have been located.[103] On the fringe of the storm, Key West had gusts of 90 miles per hour which resulted in moderate damage including $135,000 in damage to military bases onshore.[104]

The main dwelling in late 1945.

With the extra influx of younger, less trained men, lighthouse stations across the nation seemed to have a larger number of fires than usual. In late March 1945, the main dwelling at Loggerhead Key caught on fire. The building was completely gutted. A wooden kitchen directly behind the dwelling was also damaged.[67,105] The brick walls of the building were demolished several years later.[67]

After the War, a five-man crew was assigned to the station, with usually three men on the island at any one time. Under the Coast Guard, an enlisted Officer In Charge (OINC) assumed the position of head keeper.[106] Sometime after 1951 a concrete block paintlocker, fiberglass water tanks and a metal generator building were added to the station. In 1964, another fire destroyed several of the small abandoned buildings at the Carnegie Lab. By 1970, a bulb of higher intensity had increased the power of the light to two million candela.[107]

The year 1975 brought with it one of the worst tragedies Loggerhead Key Light had seen during its many years of operation. Seaman Apprentice William H. Graves came to Loggerhead Key on the Coast Guard Construction Tender ANVIL to help rebuild the eastern wharf. Only 20 years old, Graves was killed in a construction accident. A memorial plaque erected close to the wharf records "His work was of the sea and he died on her beaches just before sunset."[108]

A newspaper interview in 1982 recorded glimpses into the life of the light keepers. One keeper said "It's good duty, but it gets old after a while. ... We maintain the light which is on from sundown to sunup as a landmark for mariners, a radio beacon for ships and aircraft and we monitor the emergency channel 16 on VHF and channel 9 on CB radio." Weekly chores were assigned by the OINC including painting, mowing the lawn or special projects. The dwelling had a modern kitchen with refrigerator, microwave oven, and electric stove and oven. A big complaint was the absence of women and having to cook for each other. Water and fuel were brought in by a Coast Guard vessel once a month. Food was brought by the National Park Service boat once a week from Key West.

Off duty hours were filled with snorkeling, fishing, sunbathing, and watching TV. The station had two dogs to help with security. "Single men usually stay six weeks and then have three weeks on shore," explained the OINC, while the married men stay four weeks on then two weeks off. "The first week here is glorious, the second is all right, but the third begins to drag." The average tour of duty was 18 months.[106]

The Coast Guard Cutter HOLLYHOCK provided transportation, fuel and water to the keepers at Loggerhead Key from 1962 to 1982. The HOLLYHOCK was built for the Lighthouse Service in 1937. Decommissioned in 1982, the HOLLYHOCK was sunk as an artificial reef off Pompano Beach, FL in 1990.

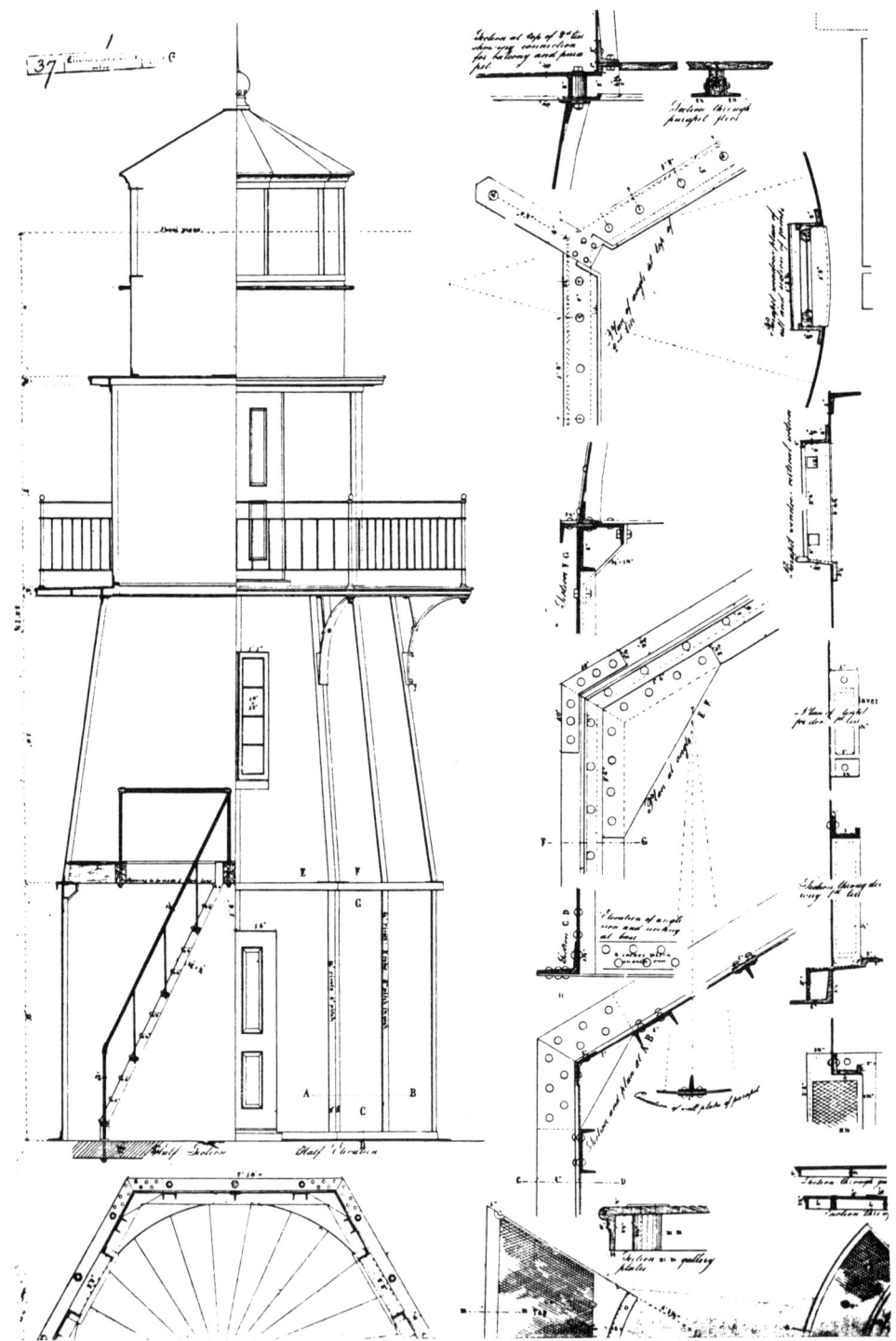

1876 plan of Garden Key Lighthouse.

Garden Key Today

Whether you come by boat or seaplane, the Dry Tortugas first appear as a low dark smudge on the horizon. If you have sharp eyes, you might see the tops of the lighthouse towers first. During the day, they appear as tiny, dark vertical lines. The larger tower on Loggerhead Key will be on the right or north, the shorter, thicker looking Garden Key tower to the left. If you arrive in the morning or afternoon, when the sun is low in the sky, it isn't until you're much closer, nearly abreast of sand bar shoals of East Key, that you can easily distinguish that Garden Key holds more than just a lighthouse.

Soon the huge brick walls are recognizable as the outline of a fort. But there's a flaw in the picture. Many of the gun ports, including nearly all of those on the second level or tier, are broken open to nearly three times the needed size. Fort Jefferson is truly a ruin, its ramparts manned by sooty terns, its vast size dwarfing the few tourists walking its walls. One can only imagine the bugle calls and drum beats that brought hundreds of men to their stations. Even easier to visualize is the loneliness and despair of the prisoners and soldiers condemned to the disease ridden fort.[109]

Fort Jefferson is open during daylight hours only. Public transportation to the fort is available from Key West by boat and seaplane. This is not your average park. The theme of the fort's isolation is strongly adhered to. There are few facilities available, so its a good idea to bring everything you might need. A primitive campground is available at no charge just outside the fort. It has grills, picnic tables and saltwater toilets, but there is no fresh water, food, supplies or bathing facilities.[55]

Garden Key Light today:

*This page: (clockwise from right)
(1) View from the lower gallery of the lighthouse, looking north.
(2) This iron ladder leads from the top of the fort's wall to the inside of the lighthouse. (3) The view from the lantern room looking towards the fort's drawbridge.*

*Facing page: (top to bottom)
(1) The exterior of the lantern where a removable wall panel opens up to the narrow upper gallery.
(2) This granite spiral staircase leads up to the base of the lighthouse. (3) A 15" Rodman cannon is on display at the base of the lighthouse (note park ranger for size comparison).
(4) The lighthouse is bolted into stonework on the top of the fort.*

National Park Service employees are on duty inside the fort, but you'll rarely see reenactments (either large or small) as there are rarely more than a few dozen visitors at the fort at any one time. Upon arrival, its a good idea to see the orientation program in the visitor center, then take the self-guided tour.

No signs mark it, but just off the self-guided tour's path is the foundation and floor of the 1828 lighthouse. It is located flush with ground-level under some trees on the parade ground near the present tower.

The foundation of the old tower.

The tour will take you up the cut granite steps of bastion 6, directly underneath the lighthouse. Except for this lower level, the interior of the lighthouse is closed to the public. Both the exterior ironwork (now painted black) and the interior wood work (painted white) of the lighthouse have been extensively restored, and are now in excellent condition. An iron ladder goes from the top of the wall through a trap door to the interior of the light. Inside, two more iron ladders lead to a trap door inside the lantern. The original lens is long gone, and its replacement, three light bulbs with glass globe coverings are purely to provide a decorative night light, not to aid navigation. A removable wall panel (facing the parade ground) provides access to the outside lantern gallery. The keeper would have used this panel when he went outside the lantern to clean its glass. Heavy wooden double doors lead to the top of the fort's wall and the railed balcony of the lighthouse.[109]

Although it was originally created to protect the massive ruins of Fort Jefferson, the National Monument's establishment has proven to be a windfall in two other respects. The National Monument's importance as a nature preserve and wildlife sanctuary is well understood, but its future may lie with man-made resources lying just under its clear blue waters. With its numerous, undisturbed wrecks, and beautiful coral reefs, the Dry Tortugas may be an important underwater laboratory for scientists of the future. Preserved by chance in the course of protecting an old fort, the shipwrecks and reefs of the Dry Tortugas may be one of the most important components of the National Monument.

Loggerhead Key Today

No seaplanes fly to Loggerhead Key, and you won't find any scheduled commercial boats to take you there either. Access to the island is strictly controlled by the Coast Guard and National Park Service. That's not to say you can't go there, you just have to get permission to go there well in advance.

The lighthouse and its wharf lay right in the middle of Loggerhead Key. The black top of the tower provides a sharp contrast to the bright skies, while the lower, white half of the tower and buildings are hidden by trees. White concrete sidewalks lead from the wharf to the lighthouse tower. The buildings at Loggerhead Key were nominated for the National Register of Historic Places in 1984. Off to the right, the foundation of the old keeper's dwelling can be seen. Nearby are two of the original brick cisterns and the "guest quarters", the converted remains of the original kitchen building. Even though it was extensively renovated in 1922, the building retains its original appearance.

Three buildings stand at the base of the lighthouse tower. A modern metal generator building provides power for the light, radiobeacon and the dwellings. At least one generator is always in operation. Attached directly to the lighthouse is the original oil storage building. Now called the radio room, this two story brick building still holds a radio, amplifier, and other supplies. Next door is the Bosun's work shop, a former oil storage building that now holds various yard tools and spare equipment.[67]

The tower itself is impressive in all aspects. A huge wooden door guards the entrance. On the bottom floor, an access hole to the central brick column has an opening to provide access to the lead weights which once turned the clockworks, spinning the lens. The inside walls are painted white and the stairs black. Because of the short width of the stairs towards the center, it is a natural tendency to use the metal handrail curving along the outside wall. Eye bolts originally held a rope that was used as a handrail, the existing metal one being a later replacement.

Loggerhead Key, tower entrance and base of stairs, 1991.

There are 216 granite steps leading up the tower, but small landings at each window provide a convenient place with wonderful views to catch your breath. Above each window sill, several large blocks of granite support the roof. Bland military stencils mark the progress past each "floor". At the top of the stairs, an I-beam frame supports the metal deck of the watchroom. This deck still has the holes and pulleys installed for the clock weight cable. The top of the central column's shaft is open to let the cable in, but the clearance between the deck and the top of the column is so narrow that another access hole is located just below the top of the column.

The watch room is almost entirely taken up by the mercury trough and revolving deck which supported the 2nd order lens. The old lens was removed in 1984 because of the mercury float. Mercury is a heavy metal that is poisonous to people. Without the mercury, the large lens won't turn. The lens was removed for safekeeping and display at the Coast Guard's Aids to Navigation School at Yorktown, Virginia. Although the lens was removed, most of its stand and turntable are still in place on Loggerhead Key. The 2nd order lens was replaced by a 24-inch range optic which looks much like a spotlight and rotates by means of an electric motor. It rotates once every 20 seconds, giving the one-sided optic the same characteristic as the old lens.

The lower balcony of the light is accessed by a iron door from the watch room. The original railing outside has been removed and replaced with a single open rail. Its not a great place for those afraid of heights. The upper lantern gallery was probably accessed by a glass door in the lantern which has since been removed. The only way to get to the upper gallery now is a potentially dangerous climb up an iron skeleton mast.

Inside the lantern room much of the original hardware still remains. Inside the domed roof a central chimney pipe stands ready to exhaust smoke from oil filled lamps. A larger funnel-like deflector surrounds the pipe to further remove soot and gasses out of the lantern room. Most of the original glass windows have been replaced with plexiglass, but brass handgrips still ring the exterior windows ready to provide grips for the keeper as he cleans salt spray from the windows. Copper pipes act as rain gutters to deflect water off the dome and away from the glass. The top of the lighthouse provides a wonderful view in all directions.

Heavy canvas curtains were once hung to inside the lantern room to block light from reaching the lens. The brass pegs which held the curtains are still present. Different sources will argue their purpose was to stop brush fires (by stopping the magnifying glass effect of the glass prisms) or to prevent the lens glass from turning green, but their actual cause was probably to prevent fires in the lantern room where volatile oils and reflected sunlight could cause a disaster.

Elsewhere on Loggerhead Key are other sites of interest. West of the lighthouse just back from the shore is the boathouse. A marine railroad once provided a means to store the station's boat inside. Now the boathouse has been converted into a recreation room. To the south, a large radio transmitter tower beams the radiobeacon's signal to ships at sea.

The northern end of the island has more historic points of interest. At the island's extreme northern end, several ruins of the Carnegie Lab can be seen. All the buildings were destroyed in a 1964 fire except a small wooden shed, the ruins of which look ready to topple into the sea in the next big storm. Concrete foundation pilings and the remains of one of the concrete specimen tanks stand nearby. The most interesting relic is a large metal plaque commemorating the lab's first director, Alfred Goldsboro Mayor. An overgrown trail on the eastern side of the island runs by the ruins of an unmortared coral rock wall. There aren't any records to

Alfred G. Mayor

One of the fascinating personalities of Loggerhead Key was the marine lab's first director, Alfred G. Mayor. Born Alfred G. Mayer in Maryland in 1868, he was raised by his father after his mother died from childbirth complications. Initially educated as a physicist to satisfy his father, he became a Harvard student in biology in 1892.

His work on butterfly pigmentation was impressive, but a serious eye inflammation forced a change in studies. Part of his eye treatment required he spend several months in a dark room. Afterwards, it was difficult for him to use microscopes. The study of jellyfish was less dependent on microscopes, so a switch was made. Mayer quickly gained prominence in his new field.

In early 1902, the Carnegie Institution of Washington DC was looking for new areas of scientific research to fund. Mayer suggested a marine laboratory and proposed the Dry Tortugas as an ideal location. The lab was approved in December 1903, with Mayer appointed as director. Since the lab was only open during the summer months, Mayer was free to make worldwide travels to other marine environments. In 1910, he published a successful three-volume edition of jellyfish of the world.

Mayer's worldwide travels and oceanographic work off Trinidad got him into trouble in 1918. He was suspected of being a German spy giving information for German submarine attacks. He was never charged, but the incident caused Mayer (who was only one-sixteenth German) to change his last name to Mayor. He spent the rest of the war in a "patriotic" position teaching navigation to Naval Officers at Princeton University. It took several years for all suspicion to end.

Mayor returned to the lab after the war but was diagnosed with tuberculous in 1921. He managed to work at the lab during the summer of 1921, but then went to a sanatorium in Tucson, Arizona. After eight months there, he was found to be nearly cured and allowed to go back to the lab for the summer 1922 season. Soon after arriving at the Tortugas, his health rapidly declined again. On June 24th, he drowned after apparently fainting while bathing alone in shallow water near the lab. He was 54. Many considered it an appropriate death for a man who loved his lab, the Tortugas and the sea so much. Mayor's wife, an accomplished sculptress, created the commemorative plaque that was erected on the island in 1923.[88]

Alfred G. Mayor

indicate when the wall was built, but inside it lies the grave of Thomas Lehay. Lehay, an ordinary seaman in the U.S. Navy, died only about three weeks after the U.S.S. Maine blew up. Lehay was not listed as a member of the Maine's crew, so it is unlikely that there is any connection between the two events.[109] One Coast Guardsman reported finding two unmarked graves at on end of the island, but the report is unconfirmed.[106]

Lehay's Grave

Fewer than 50 species of land plants are native to the Dry Tortugas. The salty soil, seasonal lack of rainfall and frequent storms limit growth. Native plants include cactus, mangrove (buttonwood), bay cedar, seagrape, sea lavender, purslane and seaoats. Starting in 1997, Park Service personnel are actively removing non-native plants including coconut palms and Australian pines which were introduced in the mid-1920's and subsequently dominated the native vegetation. [53,93]

Loggerhead Key light was officially unmanned in 1987.[110] From 1987 to the mid-1990's, Coast Guard Auxillarists served as station keepers to prevent vandalism and to help with maintenance on the generators that supplied power to the light.[111] The Coast Guard continues to maintain the lantern (a VRB-25 made by the Vega Corporation), batteries and solar panel, while the lighthouse, dwellings and island are being transferred over to National Park Service administration. Park rangers now allow visitors onto the island during the day and tours of the lighthouse itself are offered on some days.

For more than 170 years, mariners have scanned the horizon looking for this reassuring light to warn them of the dangerous reefs of the Dry Tortugas. May they always find it.

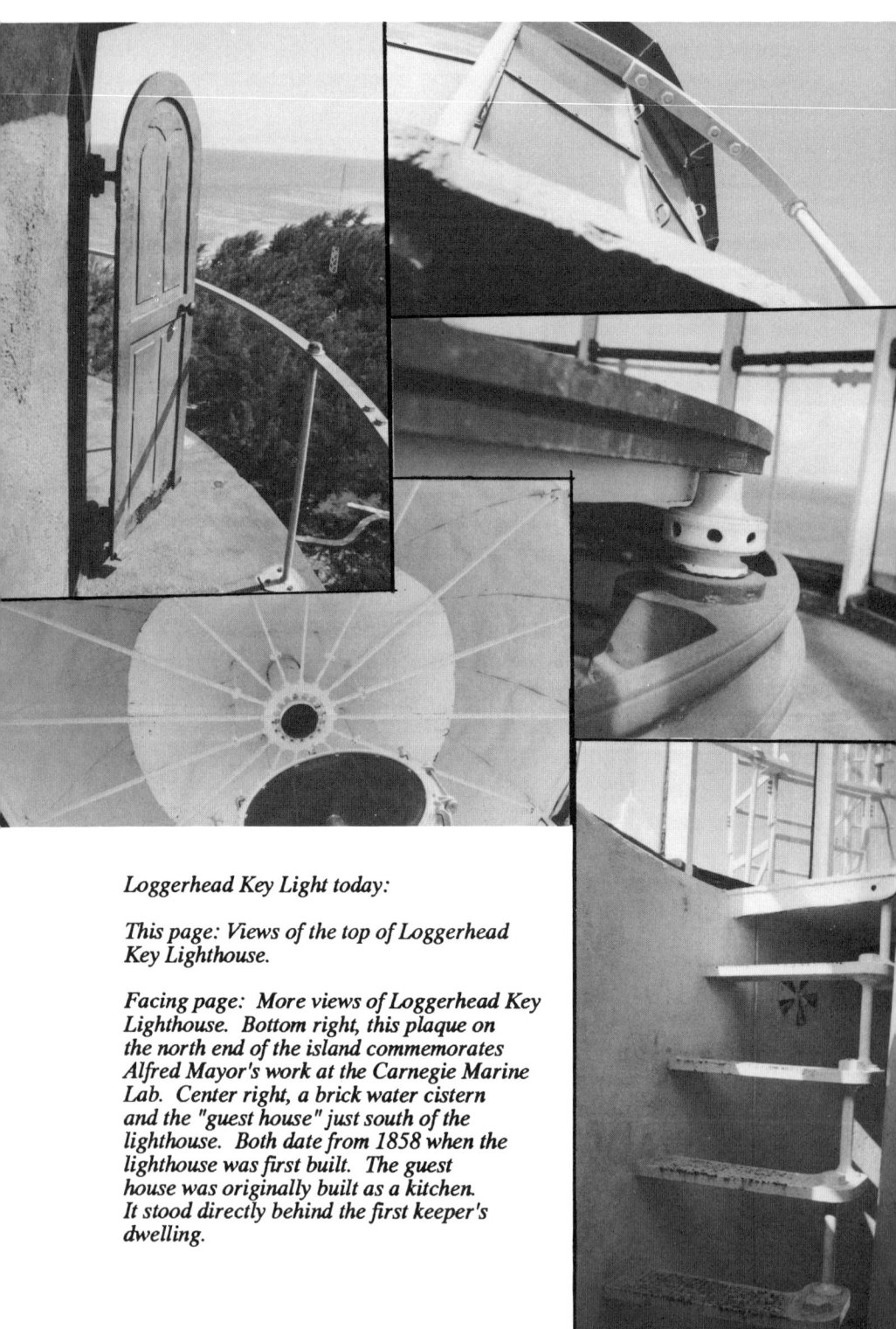

Loggerhead Key Light today:

This page: Views of the top of Loggerhead Key Lighthouse.

Facing page: More views of Loggerhead Key Lighthouse. Bottom right, this plaque on the north end of the island commemorates Alfred Mayor's work at the Carnegie Marine Lab. Center right, a brick water cistern and the "guest house" just south of the lighthouse. Both date from 1858 when the lighthouse was first built. The guest house was originally built as a kitchen. It stood directly behind the first keeper's dwelling.

PHOTO CREDITS

(front cover) 1991 photo of Loggerhead Key Lighthouse by author, (page 3) William DeBrahm's View and Profile of a Pharos, (4, 7) U. S. Lighthouse Society, (8, 9) Harper's Monthly Magazine "Along the Florida Reef" 1870–1871, (11) Frontpiece of William Whitehead's diary from Monroe County Public Library, (13) Audubon's self portrait from the National Audubon Society, (15) Harper's Monthly Magazine April 1859, (16, 18) Harper's Monthly Magazine "Along the Florida Reef" 1870–1871, (19) National Archives Record Group 26 (20) Early woodcut of the attack on Cape Florida, courtesy U.S. Lighthouse Society, (23) by author after November 1845 survey by Major Hartman Bache in National Archives Record Group 26, (28) By author after April 1847 sketch by LT H. G. Wright in National Archives Record Group 79, (29) National Archives photo in collection of the Florida State Archives, (32) After 1887 sketch by Herbert Bamber, National Archives RG 26, (33) U.S. Lighthouse Society, (34) 1862 Keeper's Implements from National Archives Record Group 26, (35) Library of Congress, (36, 37) Harper's Monthly Magazine "Along the Florida Reef" 1870–1871, (38) University of Miami, (39) original artwork by Darrell W. Orwig, (40) August 1876 "Preliminary sketch for a Cast Iron Light House" by Office of the Light House Board in National Archives Record Group 26, (41, 42 top) National Archives Record Group 26, (42 bottom) Coast Guard Historian's Office, (43) Florida State Archives from National Archives Record Group 90, (44) Florida State Archives, (46) New York Journal headlines of Feburary 17, 1898 (47 top) National Archives Record Group 26, (47 bottom) after November 1904 map of Loggerhead Key produced by the Office of the Lighthouse Engineer in the Dry Tortugas Light Station National Register Nomination, (48, 49) Carnegie Institute of Washington DC, (50) 1991 photograph by author, (51, 52) National Archives photo supplied by Mr. Rob Bethel, (53) after November 1904 map of Loggerhead Key produced by the Office of the Lighthouse Engineer in the Dry Tortugas Light Station National Register Nomination, (54–59) Coast Guard Historian's Office, (60) National Archives Record Group 79, (61–66) 1991 photographs by author, (68) Carnegie Institute of Washington DC, (69–71) 1991 photographs by author, (back cover) 1991 photo of Garden Key Lighthouse, by author.

SPECIAL THANKS

The generous assistance of the following people made this book possible: Mr. Michael Eng and Mr. Cliff Green of the National Park Service; Mr. Tom Hambright, local historian for Monroe County Public Library; Mr. Wayne Wheeler of the United States Lighthouse Society; the members of Coast Guard Aids To Navigation Team Key West; the Florida State Archives Still Pictures Branch; Mr. Ray Bowers of the Carnegie Institute of Washington DC; Mr. Rob Bethel; LTJG Darrell Orwig, USCGR; and Dr. Robert Browning and Mr. Kevin Foster from the Coast Guard Historian's Office.

FOOTNOTES

A Dangerous Obstacle
(1) Works Progress Administration, "A Guide to Key West" (Hastings House NY 1949)
(2) Fort Jefferson National Monument "General Management Plan Development, Concept Plan Environmental Assessment" (March 1983)
(3) Bearss, Edwin C., "Fort Jefferson National Monument Florida, Shipwreck Study, The Dry Tortugas" (National Park Service 1971)
(4) Markham, Clements R., "Hawkins' Voyages During the Reigns of Henry VIII, Elizabeth and James I" (The Haulkut Society, London 1875)
(5) Wood, Peter, "The Spanish Main, The Seafarers" (Time-Life Books, Alexandria VA 1979)
(6) Swanson, C. Gail, "Dutch at Dry Torugas", (Florida Keys Sea Heritage Journal, Vol 2 #1, Fall 1991, Key West Maritime Historical Society)
(7) Fort Jefferson National Monument "Historic Structure Report, Historical Data Section, Fort Jefferson: 1846-1898" (National Park Service July 1983)
(8) Holder, Joseph B., "The Dry Tortugas" (Harper's Monthly Magazine June 1868)
(9) De Vorsey, Louis, "De Brahm's Report of the General Survey in the Southern district of North America" (University of South Carolina Press, Columbia SC, 1971)

Building the Lighthouse
(10) Carter, Clarence K., "The Territorial Papers of the United States" (GPO Washington, DC 1965)
(11) National Archives "Lighthouse Contracts" (Record Group 26)
(12) CIS U.S. Serial Set (Records of Congress) Serial 131, Document 19, 1825
(13) Pinkney to Pleasonton, April 27, 1826 "Letters Received, Department of Treasury" (National Archives Record Group 26)
(14) Light List 1844 (GPO Washington DC)
(15) Bache, Major Hartman, "Map of Garden Key of the Tortugas Group 1845" (National Archives Record Group 26)
(16) Conant, Rodger, "A Field Guide to Reptiles and Amphibians of Eastern and Central North America", (Houghton Mifflin Co. Boston 1975)
(17) Botting, Douglas, "The Seafarers Series: The Pirates" (Time-Life Books, Alexandria, VA 1978)
(18) Holder, Joseph B., "Along the Florida Reef" (Harpers Monthly Magazine Dec 1870-May 1871)
(19) Adams, Alexander B., "John James Audubon, A Biography", (G.P. Putnam's Sons NY 1966)

A Hard Life
(20) Pinkney to Pleasonton, October 1, 1826 "Letters Received, Department of Treasury" (National Archives Record Group 26)
(21) Pinkney to Pleasonton, November 3, 1826 "Letters Received, Department of Treasury" (National Archives Record Group 26)
(22) Doane to Coste, November 19, 1826 "Letters Received, Department of Treasury" (Record Group 26)

(23) Pinkney to Pleasonton, November 30, 1826 "Letters Received, Department of Treasury" (National Archives Record Group 26)
(24) Pinkney to Pleasonton, December 3, 1826 "Letters Received, Department of Treasury" (National Archives Record Group 26)
(25) Pinkney to Pleasonton, March 8, 1827 "Letters Received, Department of Treasury" (National Archives Record Group 26)
(26) Pinkney to Pleasonton, April 23, 1827 "Letters Received, Department of Treasury" (National Archives Record Group 26)
(27) Pinkney to Pleasonton, October 20, 1826 "Letters Received, Department of Treasury" (National Archives Record Group 26)
(28) Pinkney to Pleasonton May 13, 1828 "Letters Received, Department of Treasury" (National Archives Record Group 26)
(29) Dean, Love, "The Loggerhead Light", (Florida Keys Magazine, Jan c. 1981-1984)
(30) Whitehead to Pleasonton August 21, 1833 "Letters Received, Department of Treasury" (National Archives Record Group 26)
(31) Whitehead to Pleasonton May 18, 1835 "Letters Received, Department of Treasury" (National Archives Record Group 26)
(32) Shepard, Birse, "Lore of the Wreckers" (Beacon Press, Boston, 1961)
(33) Whitehead to Pleasonton, April 1, 1834 "Letters Received, Department of Treasury" (National Archives Record Group 26)
(34) Pinkney to Pleasonton, August 20, 1827 "Letters Received, Department of Treasury" (National Archives Record Group 26)
(35) Himinez to Pinkney, August 28, 1827 "Letters Received, Department of Treasury" (National Archives Record Group 26)
(36) Hurley, Neil E., "Keeper's of Florida Lighthouses 1820-1939" (Historic Lighthouse Publishers, Alexandria VA 1990)
(37) Pinkney to Pleasonton, July 1, 1828 "Letters Received, Department of Treasury" (National Archives Record Group 26)
(38) Paine to Pinkney, August 6, 1830 "Letters Received, Department of Treasury" (National Archives Record Group 26)
(39) Whitehead to Pleasonton, June 4, 1831 "Letters Received, Department of Treasury" (National Archives Record Group 26)
(40) Whitehead to Pleasonton, April 5, 1832 "Letters Received, Department of Treasury" (National Archives Record Group 26)
(41) Whitehead to Pleasonton, February 10, 1836 "Letters Received, Department of Treasury" (National Archives Record Group 26)
(42) Adams, Alexander B., "John James Audubon, a Biography" (G. P. Putnam's Sons, NY 1966)

The Wreck of the AMERICA
(43) Whitehead to Pleasonton, November 10, 1836 "Letters Received by the Treasury Department" (National Archives Record Group 26)

Temporary Fixes
(44) Whitehead to Pleasonton, December 31, 1836 "Letters Received by the Department of Treasury" (National Archives Record Group 26)
(45) Hurley, Neil E., "An Illustrated History of Cape Florida Lighthouse" (Historic Lighthouse Publishers, Camino CA 1989)

(46) Whitehead to Pleasonton, July 1, 1837 "Letters Received by the Department of Treasury" (National Archives Record Group 26)
(47) Whitehead or Gordon to Pleasonton, May 11, 1838 "Letters Received by the Department of Treasury" (National Archives Record Group 26)
(48) Gordon to Pleasonton, August 13, 1838 "Letters Received by the Department of Treasury" (National Archives Record Group 26)
(49) Gordon to Pleasonton, June 16, 1840 "Letters Received by the Department of Treasury" (National Archives Record Group 26)
(50) Gordon to Pleasonton, September 6, 1842 "Letters Received by the Department of Treasury" (National Archives Record Group 26)
(51) Gordon to Pleasonton, October 4, 1842 "Letters Received by the Department of Treasury" (National Archives Record Group 26)
(52) Gordon to Pleasonton, December 22, 1842 "Letters Received by the Department of Treasury" (National Archives Record Group 26)
(53) Gordon to Pleasonton, September 12, 1842 "Letters Received by the Department of Treasury" (National Archives Record Group 26)
(54) Gordon to Pleasonton, January 6, 1843 "Letters Received by the Department of Treasury" (National Archives Record Group 26)

New Neighbors and the Great Escape
(55) Fort Jefferson National Monument, brochure entitled "Fort Jefferson National Monument Florida" (National Park Service, GPO 1991)
(56) Bethel, Rodman "A Slumbering Giant of the Past, Fort Jefferson, U.S.A. in the Dry Tortugas" (By author, Key West FL 1989)
(57) Wright to Totten, Monthly report for July 1847 "Letters Received by the War Department" (National Archives Record Group 77)
(58) Whitehurst to Wright, July 12, 1847 "Letters Received by the Office of Chief of Engineers" (National Archives Record Group 77)
(59) Wright to Totten, July 21, 1847 "Letters Received by the Office of Chief of Engineers" (National Archives Record Group 77)
(60) Cooper, James Fenimore, "Jack Tier; or The Florida Reef" (first published in Graham's Magazine (Nov 1846–Mar 1848) as "The Islets of the Gulf; or Rose Budd". In 1848 it was published as "Jack Tier ..." by Burgess, Stringer and Company. The British title was "Captain Spike; or The Islets of the Gulf")

A New Light
(61) Key West Collector to Pleasonton, July 10, 1845 "Letters Received by the Department of Treasury" (National Archives Record Group 26)
(62) Wheeler, Wayne, "History of the Administration of the U.S. Light House Service" (The Keeper's Log Magazine, Spring 1989)
(63) Report of LT John Rodgers "Annual Report of the Coast Survey 1851" (House Document 26)
(64) Young to the Light-House Board, April 1852 "Report of the Light-House Board" (CIS U.S. Serial Set Index serial 648, document 114)
(65) Dry Tortugas Light Station, FL "Clip Files" (National Archives, Record Group 26)
(66) Sifakis, Steward, "Who Was Who in the Civil War" (Facts on File Publications, NY 1988)
(67) National Register of Historic Places Inventory-Nomination Form (1984)

(68) Lighthouse Implements, Plans from 1862 (National Archives Record Group 26)
(69) Dean, Love, "Reef Lights, Seaswept Lighthouses of the Florida Keys", (Key West Historic Preservation Board 1982)

The Fort Becomes a Prison

(70) Manucy, Albert C., "The History of Fort Jefferson National Monument" (Florida Works Progress Administration 1936)
(71) Carter, Samuel, "The Riddle of Dr. Mudd" (G.P. Putnam's Sons, New York 1974)
(72) Cleaves, Freeman, "Meade of Gettysburg" (University of Oklahoma Press, 1960)
(73) "Sun, Sand and Soldiers, the Diary of SGT H.B. Herrick", (Oswego County Historical Society 1953)
(74) Williams, Joy, "The Florida Keys, a History and Guide From Key Largo to Key West" (Random House, NY 1987)
(75) Light List 1899 (GPO Washington DC)

Hurricanes and Repairs

(76) Photo c. 1880 of Fort Point Lighthouse CA (U.S. Coast Guard Historian's Office)
(77) Light list 1908 (GPO Washington DC)
(78) Marx, Robert F., "Shipwrecks in Florida Waters" (Scott Publishing Co., Eau Gallie FL 1969)
(79) Rebecca Shoal "Clip Files" (Record Group 26, National Archives)
(80) Light lists 1935-1987 (GPO Washington, DC)

Quiet Times Despite War

(81) Fort Jefferson Buoy Depot "Clip Files" (National Archives Record Group 26)
(82) Davis, Burke, et al. "200 Years, A Bicentennial Illustrated History of the United States" (U.S. News and World Report, Washington DC 1973)
(83) O'Toole, G.J.A., "The Spanish War, An American Epic 1898" (W. W. Norton, New York 1984)
(84) Rickover, H.G., "How the Battleship Maine was Destroyed" (GPO, Washington, DC, 1976)
(85) Light list 1902 (GPO Washington DC)

The End of and Era

(86) Holland, Francis R., "America's Lighthouses, An Illustrated History" (Dover Publications Inc., 1988)
(87) Carnegie Institution Yearbooks
(88) Colin, Patrick L., "Love Not Logic" (unpublished manuscript held by the Carnegie Institute, 1974)
(89) England, George A., "Isles of Romance" (The Century Co., NY 1929)
(90) Lighthouse Bureau "Report 60, Description of Light Station for the Dry Tortugas" (National Archives Record Group 26)
(91) Light List 1914 (GPO Washington DC)
(92) Light List 1922 (GPO Washington DC)

Flashing Lights

(93) "Logbook for Dry Tortugas Lightstation 1925-1933" (National Archives, Record Group 26)
(94) U.S. Light House Service Monthly Bulletin 1923 (Department of Commerce, GPO)
(95) "Light Keepers Generously Supplied with Radio Receiving Sets" U.S. Light House Service Monthly Bulletins 1929 (Department of Commerce, GPO)
(96) Light list 1934 (GPO Washington DC)
(97) U.S. Coast Guard "Luminous Intensities of Aids to Navigation Light" (COMDTINST M16510.2, 1984)
(98) U.S. Light House Service Monthly Bulletins 1934 & 1935 (Department of Commerce, GPO)
(99) U.S. Light House Service Monthly Bulletins 1938 (Department of Commerce, GPO)
(100) U.S. Coast Guard, Historical Section "The Coast Guard at War, Volume 15, Aids to Navigation" (GPO 1944)
(101) U.S. Coast Guard "Request for Work Authorization 08 May 1942" (Unpublished, filed with Aids to Navigation Records in the Seventh Coast Guard District)
(102) The Miami Herald, "All of South Florida Under Hurricane Alert" (Oct 18, 1944)
(103) U.S. Department of Commerce, NOAA, "Some Devastating North Atlantic Hurricanes of the 20th Century" (GPO Washington DC, 1977)
(104) Michler, D. R., "Key West in World War II, A History of the Naval Station and Naval Operations Base" (Report held by Monroe County Public Library, September 1945)
(105) U.S. Coast Guard, "photos dated April 4, 1945" (Unpublished, Coast Guard Historian's Office)
(106) Platero, John, "Loneliness is a Large Part of Lighthouse Duty" (The Bridgeport Sunday Post, December 12, 1982)
(107) Light List 1970 (GPO Washington DC)
(108) Plaque on Loggerhead Key

Garden Key Today

(109) Site visit, August 1991
(110) Wheeler, Wayne, "And Then There Were None" (The Keeper's Log, Summer 1987)
(111) Maloney, James, "Lighthouse Keeping" (U.S. Coast Guard Auxiliary Magazine "The Navigator", Summer 1990)

Loggerhead Key Today

(none)

This inscription plate, designed for a replacement tower at Loggerhead Key, was never made.

THE AUTHOR

"Lighthouses of the Dry Tortugas" is Neil Hurley's third book dealing with the history of Florida Lighthouses. His interest began over ten years ago as he serviced Great Lakes lighthouses while assigned to the Coast Guard Buoy Tender SUNDEW. At his next assignment, on the staff of the Aids to Navigation Branch of the Seventh Coast Guard District in Miami, he responded to questions from the public about lighthouses in Florida. While there, he was surprised to find out that no detailed history of lighthouses in Florida existed.

Taking matters into his own hands, Neil scoured records from the Coast Guard, National Archives and various historical organizations for first-hand information on each lighthouse. His first book, "An Illustrated History of Cape Florida Lighthouse" included previously unpublished details surrounding the 1836 Indian attack which destroyed the lighthouse. His second book, "Keepers of Florida Lighthouses 1826-1939" contains the names, dates of service and other information on the more than 1,000 lighthouse keepers who served in Florida. Neil is also the author of several articles in the U. S. Lighthouse Society magazine "The Keeper's Log".

Now a Lieutenant Commander, Neil is assisgned to Coast Guard Marine Safety Office Honolulu where he develops and admisters Oil Spill Response plans. He and his wife Jackie have two sons, Caleb and Seth. He's currently working on a book to be titled "A History of Lighthouses on Cape Canaveral" and a book detailing the history of all of Florida's lighthouses.

INDEX

ACTIVA 25, 29, 30, 31
Adams, John Qunicy 10
Adare, Johnny 37
Aids to Navigation School 66
Akin, Lemuel S. 15,17
ALFRED 12
Alligator Reef Light, FL 55
AMERICA 15, 17
AMESBURY 31
ANTON DOHRN 49
ANVIL 58
Appleby, Joshua 11
Arnold, Major 36
Audubon, John 8, 13
AURORA 43
Beaty, Mr. 22
Benner, Keeper 35
Bethel, Joseph 22
Bethel, Nicholosa 22
bird life 2, 13, 29, 48, 49, 56
Blank, Harry 37
Booth, John Wilkes 38
Budd, Rose 26,27
CANTON 29, 30
Cape Florida Light, FL 19, 20
CARIBOU 43
CARMILITA COMPOSITE 45
Carnegie Lab (see Marine Lab)
carrier pigeons 56, 57
Carter, Aaron 19, 20
Chase, Captain 29
Civil War 31, 35, 36, 42
Coast Guard 54, 57-59, 65, 66
Coast Guard Auxiliary 69
Commerce, Department of 47
CONCORD 16
Cooper, James Fenimore 26
Day, Captain 29
De Brahm, William 2, 3, 4
Dubose, John 20
Dunn, James 36, 37
Dutton, Captain 29
Eagan, James 13
electricity 55, 56
English, Jack 28
English, W. F. 28
fevers and tropical disease 7, 9, 24, 37-40, 43-45
Franklin, Samuel 10
fires 20, 46, 51, 52, 58, 67

Flaherty, John L. 9-11
Flaherty, Rebecca 9-11
Fletcher, Robert R. 19, 21
FLORENCE 13, 16
fog 1, 12, 39, 30
Fort Barrancas 29
Fort Jefferson 24, 28, 31, 35-38, 40, 45, 46, 49, 51, 54, 61
Fort Jefferson National Monument 8, 42, 54, 64
Fort McRea 29
Fort Pickens 29
Fort Point Lighthouse, CA 41
Fort Winfield Scott, CA 41
Fresh water 2, 6, 7, 12, 23, 25, 27, 54, 59, 61
Fresnel lenses 30, 32, 33, 50, 53
Fritz, John 33
Gauld, George 2
Glover, Edward 12, 13, 16
Graves, William H. 58
Hall, Keeper 54
Havana, Cuba 2
Hawkins, John 1, 2
Hillsboro Inlet Light, FL 39
Himinez, Joseph 10, 11, 12
HOLLYHOCK 59
Hoover, Herbert 55
Humphries, Noah 7
Hurricanes 11, 22, 24, 26, 31, 39-41, 43, 47-52, 57
Jack Tier (book) 26, 27
JOSEPH R. PARROTT 56
Kerr, Benjamin H. 33, 35
Knowlton, Mr. 21
LEGAR 29
Lehay, Thomas 69
Lehman, George 13
Lester, Mr. 28
Lewis, Winslow 9
Lighthouse:
  Board 30, 31, 40, 45, 47
  Bureau of, 47
  contracts 5, 6, 32
  first lighting 7, 33, 41, 42
  mercury float for, 66
  site of first, 64
  visibility of 56
Lincoln, Samuel B., 5, 6
Lincoln, Abraham 36, 38

LORETO 15, 17
MAINE 46, 69
Marine Lab (Carnegie Lab) 47–49, 51, 67, 68
MARION 9, 13
Mason, Jerry 28
Mayor, Alfred Goldsboro 67, 68
Meade, George 42
Mobile, AL 15, 56
Mobile Point Light, AL 19
MOLLY SWASH 26
Mudd, Samuel 38
Mulford, Harry 26, 27
National Park Service 54, 59, 61, 64, 65, 69
NEW YORK 22
Niell, Captain 11
Nordhoff, Charles 15,17
NUESTRA SENORA DEL ROSARIO 2
Oliver, Captain 12
Perry, Charles H. 33
Pinkney, William 9, 10, 11, 12
Ponce de Leon, Juan 1
Porter, David 6, 23
POUGHKEEPSIE 26
Prisoners 36, 37, 38
Pulaski Shoal Light, FL 42
Radio 53–55, 57, 58, 65
Radiobeacon 42, 54, 55, 57, 58, 65, 67
Rebecca Shoal Light FL 42
Rickover, Hyman G. 46
Rodgers, John 23
Sand Key Light, FL 10,11,22
Saywer, Ben 17, 18
Seminole Indians 19, 20
Slaves 19, 20, 25, 28, 30
Smith, Elliot 12
SOUTH CAROLINA 12
Spanish American War 45, 46
SPERMACETI 16
Spike, Steven 26, 27
SUN 56

Tennessee Reef Light, FL 42
Thompson 18, 25, 28, 30
Thompson, Alexander 13
Thompson, John 22
Thompson, John (slave) 25, 30
Thompson, John W. B. 19, 20
treasure 2, 35
torture 36, 37
Turtles 1, 2, 8, 24, 27
Treasury Department 30
Tyler, John 24
UNION 25
UNITED STATES 12
Van Evans, Edward 11
VICTOR 25, 28
VIRGINIA 25
Wan, Don 27
Ward, Henry 13
WILLIAM S. FARWELL 44
WYANDOTTE 36
World War I 68
World War II 57
Woodbury, Daniel P. 31
Wright, Horatio 24, 28, 31

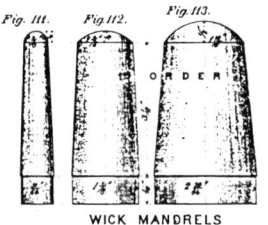

WICK MANDRELS